T0283067

EVERYDAY
DHARMA

EVERYDAY DHARMA

8 ESSENTIAL PRACTICES FOR FINDING SUCCESS AND JOY IN EVERYTHING YOU DO

SUNEEL GUPTA

HARPERONE

An Imprint of HarperCollins*Publishers*

HarperCollins books may be purchased for educational, business, or sales promotional use. For information, please email the Special Markets Department at SPsales@harpercollins.com.

FIRST EDITION

Ashoka wheel © Azaan Alam/Shutterstock
Photograph on page 171 courtesy of the author

Library of Congress Cataloging-in-Publication Data has been applied for.

ISBN 978-0-06-314387-6

23 24 25 26 27 LBC 5 4 3 2 1

THIS BOOK IS DEDICATED TO MY ANCESTORS . . .

AND TO YOURS

The stories inside this book are deeply personal to the people who lived them. In some cases, names and identifying characteristics have been changed to protect their privacy.

CONTENTS

WHERE WE BEGIN

If you look hard enough at your own story, you'll find a moment that feels like the true beginning. For me, it's sitting on the porch of my dad's childhood home in New Delhi.

I'm seven years old and I'm seated next to my seventy-two-year-old grandfather. My *bauji* is legendarily large for an Indian man, barrel-chested and bald. Back home in Detroit, a portrait of him hung near our hallway closet. He wasn't smiling, but there was warmth and wisdom to his gaze. The confidence of a caretaker.

Over the past month, Bauji and I spent each morning together on this porch, his bare feet firmly pressed into the ground, mine dangling from my chair. Together, we watched the streets of Delhi come alive: the fruit cart vendors bellowing prices into the open air, cows ambling toward their pasture, rickshaws cranking their diesel engines to begin their commutes.

On that porch, Bauji shared lessons that would take me decades to unpack and absorb. Lessons I had forgotten, then rediscovered when I needed them most, at a point in my life when I didn't understand who I was. When I felt lost, angry, and seriously burnt out.

There's an urgency to Bauji this morning. In a couple of hours, my parents and I will be catching a flight back to the United States. And there seems to be one final lesson that my grandfather wants to impart.

Bauji raises a large hand and points to an Indian flag raised from a structure down the street. "You see the center of the flag, *beta?*" he asks, calling me "son" the way my parents do.

I gaze in the direction of his finger and notice the orange, white, and green banner gently blowing in the wind. At the heart of the flag is a navy blue wheel.

"That's the Ashoka Chakra," says Bauji. "The Wheel of Dharma."

Bauji begins to draw the shape of a wheel in the air. He traces and retraces its perimeter, each time picking up speed. He draws faster and faster until he's maniacally rounding the circle. His seriousness has shifted to play, his eyes are smiling. I let out a giggle, and he unleashes a giant belly laugh that I'm sure will wake my cousins sleeping inside.

My grandfather takes a long sip of his hot chai, and I watch the steam rise from the mug and slightly fog his large-framed glasses. He removes them and I see what look like tiny tears welling at the corners of his dark brown eyes.

Perhaps Bauji knew that this would be the last time we'd ever see each other.

He tells me that as I get older, the wheel will move faster. Time will accelerate. Years will squish together. Each birthday will arrive a little sooner than the one before. And as the wheel turns faster and faster, life will pull me to the outside, away from who I really am at my core. Away from my *Dharma*.

That's when Bauji takes a deep breath and begins the journey that you and I are about to take together.

"Beta," he says for the final time, "you must find your way back to the center."

♦ ♦ ♦

When I was in seventh grade, I believed my dharma was to be a speechwriter. I wrote speeches for friends, family members, and classmates. If you needed a speech for a birthday, wedding, or bar mitzvah, I was your guy. I didn't get paid for any of this, but I loved every minute.

As I got older, I took on part-time jobs and internships writing for local leaders. I moved to Washington, DC, and wrote for congressmen and even presidential candidates. Writing speeches tapped into something deep inside of me. When I woke up in the morning, I felt energized and ready to tackle the day. It was a feeling I wanted to hold on to, the kind of work I wanted to devote the rest of my life to.

A few years later, though, I found myself being lured in a different direction. The iPhone had just launched, social media companies were taking off, and tech entrepreneurs were becoming billionaires overnight. Suddenly it seemed like all my friends were moving to Silicon Valley to be part of the action.

I felt torn between two worlds: one I knew I loved and another I was afraid to miss.

Ultimately, the financial allure of Silicon Valley was just too much for me to pass up. I moved out there with the dream of becoming a successful entrepreneur. And after a few years of working for other tech companies, I decided it was time to start my own.

My first startup failed, and so did my second. When I decided to give it one more try, I felt that everything was on the line: my pride, my dignity, and my dwindling bank account. For the next several years, I bootstrapped my life, took a zero-dollar salary, and worked harder than I ever had before.

It was a high-stress existence, and the pressure took a toll. I was constantly sick, stressed out, and sleep-deprived. It became more and more difficult to get out of bed in the morning.

I told myself it didn't matter because once I'd made my dream a reality—once I finally had the success, status, and wealth I was after—the joy would return and the emptiness I was feeling would fade away.

And then it happened. My startup RISE was acquired by a large healthcare company. Suddenly, I had money in the bank. I was being profiled by CNBC and the *Wall Street Journal*. I was asked to speak about RISE's success at conferences. It all felt euphoric.

But a couple of weeks after the sale, I woke up to a sinking realization: those good feelings had disappeared. In fact, I didn't feel any happier than I had before.

I was having trouble making sense of it. This was supposed to be *my moment*. The one that made all the years of hard work and sacrifice feel worthwhile. The moment when everything would finally be okay. Instead, I felt emptier than ever before. I genuinely believed that something was broken inside of me.

That's when I began to remember the lessons Bauji taught me so many years before. I found myself transported back to his porch in New Delhi, staring at the Indian flag and the Wheel of

Dharma. I realized then that I had drifted to the outside of the wheel.

My grandfather's voice became clear: "You must find your way back to the center."

◆ ◆ ◆

We've been conditioned, from an early age, to believe that one day we'll reach a moment of "arrival." Get good grades, go to a good school, get a good job, make good money, and we'll be fulfilled. Even as we get older, and realize that life isn't quite so simple, we still manage to convince ourselves that if we can just get that next sale, next job, next promotion—*then* we'll finally be happy.

Dr. Tal Ben-Shahar at Harvard University calls this the "arrival fallacy." Every time you hit a target that's supposed to bring you lasting joy, the goalpost moves again. And when the chase is never-ending, when we are constantly in pursuit of a feeling we can't quite obtain, our tank inevitably runs out of gas. We become exhausted, we burn out. And we quietly start to question the purpose of it all.

Because if outer success (wealth, status, achievement) isn't leading us to a feeling of inner success (joy, fulfillment, personal growth), then what's the point? What's the purpose of hard work and ambition if getting what we want only leads us back to the emotional place we were in before?

A few years ago, I began to realize that I wasn't the only one who felt this way. Nearly everywhere I looked, people seemed lost and angry. Lost because if there is no point of arrival, then where the hell are we on the map? Angry because we went to school, took out loans, got jobs, showed up every day, and did all the things we were supposed to do—only to find that we were no closer to the sense of joy that we had been chasing all these years.

So a lot of us checked out. We disengaged. We quit quietly or left our jobs. When this happened en masse, they called it the "Great Resignation." Experts went on television to argue that it was a flash in the pan, a ripple effect of the COVID-19 pandemic. What they didn't understand is that this sense of dissatisfaction had been building long before the virus disrupted our lives.

In 2015, a joint working paper from Stanford and Harvard reported that health problems arising from workplace anxiety accounted for more deaths each year than diabetes or Alzheimer's disease. And in 2019, the World Health Organization included "burnout" in its International Classification of Diseases, naming it an "occupational phenomenon."

For too long, we have fixated on the future of work and ignored the future of *worth*. For too long, we've dismissed "joy" as being too flimsy to fit into a place of business. And for too long, we've assumed that outer success will lead to inner success, despite history proving again and again that this has never been the case.

In fact, more than a thousand years before the Great Resignation, there was another exodus from the workforce: a movement my ancestors called the Great Renunciation.

◆ ◆ ◆

Imagine ancient India, a golden era. Cities and commerce and marketplaces were all emerging. Brightly colored carriages packed the streets. Elephants elegantly transported merchandise to and from distant lands.

You could hear, smell, and feel progress everywhere. Huts turned into homes, tattered sheets gave way to finely stitched clothing, and dirt floors converted to marble. Companies began to form. Entrepreneurs hustled their way out of poverty. Employees embraced workweeks.

It was exciting, and yet it didn't take folks long to feel the grind. Promotions led to more responsibility; hard work led to more hard work. Parents struggled to spend time with their children. Neighbors began to feel like strangers. Communities became overrun by a tone of competitiveness. Emotional exhaustion filled the air.

This opened up what some refer to as a "spiritual vacuum" in South Asia. People were achieving more than ever before, and yet feeling no greater sense of fulfillment in their everyday lives.

Spirited debates broke out across the subcontinent. One side pointed to the buildings and the markets and said, "Look how far we've come!" The other side responded with, "Yes, but are we any happier as a result?"

The divide deepened over time. One camp came to represent outer success and the other came to represent inner success. One side championed the creation of wealth and status; the other began a quest for meaning and joy. They renounced their material possessions and quit their jobs. Many fled to the forests in search of stillness. Their goal was to return to the simpler times of their ancestors. Deep in nature—and far from the grind—they were free to meditate, pray, and rejoice in a feeling of liberation.

After a while, though, all that free time felt like *too much* free time. People began to *miss* the outside world. Not necessarily the pressure and the pace—but the act of creating, building, and getting things done. They missed serving their customers and their community. They missed waking up with a sense of purpose and going to bed with a sense of accomplishment.

The forest dwellers knew the working world led to burnout—but escaping it led to boredom. It was anxiety versus apathy. Neither felt like a good way to live.

So they went searching for a middle path, one that didn't force them to choose between outer ambition and inner peace. They wanted both: to dream big *and* to feel fulfilled.

The principles that emerged changed everything. People began to reach new heights on the outside, while experiencing a more lasting sense of joy on the inside. To them, outer success and inner success no longer felt like spiritual opposites—they were connected at the core.

Over generations, this middle path shaped extraordinary lives around the planet. It traveled from the East to the West, from ancient times to the modern day. But the name has always stayed the same.

DHARMA

Dharma is a Sanskrit word loaded with meaning. Its definition has been interpreted by communities around the world, from Buddhist monasteries to Burning Man camps. For your journey ahead, we are going straight to the source. To the most ancient and storied scripture on dharma, the Hindu book of living—the Bhagavad Gita.

The Bhagavad Gita says that each of us has a dharma, or a

"sacred duty." Duty to whom, exactly? To the fire burning inside of you. Some call this purpose, others call it your gift. My grandfather called it your *essence.*

Bauji believed that we all have an essence, something inside of us that was uniquely assigned by the universe. This goes deeper than talent or skill. It's a calling. An inner necessity.

Your essence doesn't care about power, promotions, or possessions. It only cares about one thing: expression.

If essence is who you really are, then *expression* is how you show up in the world. Your essence is always calling for you—expression is how you take that call.

There's a saying in the Gospel of Thomas: If you bring forth what is within you, that thing will save you. If you don't, it will destroy you. That's the thing about your essence. It is an inner flame that either lights up the world around you or burns a hole inside of you.

Each of us gets to choose between expression or emptiness. But no one escapes that choice.

It's pretty simple, really. When you're expressing your essence, you're in your dharma. You come alive in a brand-new way. You feel confident, creative, and caring. You are no longer asking for permission to do what you love. You are serving others with energy and kindness.

And you are experiencing true joy—not just from the goals you hit, but from the actions you take.

After my inner flame went dark, I went searching for a spark. I began digging into the stories of people who had rediscovered their essence. I saw how the principles of dharma were written about by Viktor Frankl, preached by Dr. Martin Luther King, and practiced by Mahatma Gandhi. How the qualities of dharma could be found in Hank Aaron's swing, Toni Morrison's novels, and Jimi Hendrix's songs.

I went back to India, to where my ancestors first uncovered their essence. Sitting on Bauji's old porch, I watched the streets of Delhi come alive. I reflected on the lessons he taught me all those years ago. And I put that wisdom to work, using it to finally find my way back to the center of the wheel.

Inside this book are the eight most powerful practices I've discovered on this journey. Without them, I would have remained lost, angry, and burnt out.

I learned firsthand that outer success rarely leads to inner success. But when you begin with inner success—when you start by expressing your essence—you are on a clear path to outer success as well.

This is what the people in those forests came to understand thousands of years ago. You don't have to renounce your ambitions, dreams, or goals. You don't have to flee your work in order to find happiness. You can find joy in the work itself.

Whether you're looking to change your career, reset your way of life, or strengthen what you already have, this book is designed to help you reconnect with your essence and live from that place every single day. A place where you'll be free to follow your wildest dreams, produce your life's work, and experience true joy along the way.

CHAPTER ONE

SUKHA

UNCOVERING YOUR ESSENCE

My grandfather's crinkled copy of the Bhagavad Gita was always resting on his bed stand. I remember sneaking into his room one night and asking him to read me a story from the book. It was past my bedtime, sure, but this was a request Bauji simply couldn't refuse.

He placed his reading glasses on the bridge of his nose, cracked the binding of the ancient text, and began to tell me the story of a young and handsome hero named Arjuna.

Arjuna is in the back seat of a chariot, on his way to battle. Good and evil are about to clash, and with Arjuna leading the way, the forces of good expect a resounding victory. There's just one small catch:

Arjuna is in the middle of a panic attack.

Staring at the forces that oppose him, he becomes overwhelmed with feelings of doubt. He questions his purpose, his identity, and his mission. In this moment of desperation and despair, Arjuna crumbles to the floor of his chariot.

This is Arjuna's moment to shine—to do his greatest work—and yet he feels paralyzed by insecurity. In a last-ditch effort to pull himself together, Arjuna turns to his charioteer for help.

This is when he learns that his humble servant is actually Krishna—the god of protection, compassion, and love. Krishna pulls Arjuna to his feet, but the warrior can't look his charioteer in the eyes. Staring at the ground, he shamefully admits that he's lost. That he doesn't know what to do or how to act.

Krishna responds with a single line that will inform the rest of our journey into dharma. Powerful words that get to the heart of how we feel when something is missing but we don't know why. Krishna says:

"You do not know how to act because you do not know who you are."

◆ ◆ ◆

Dharma = essence + expression.

Your essence is who you are. Your expression is how you show up in the world. Your essence is your calling, and your expression is how you take that call. My ancestors had another word for essence. They called it *Sukha* (pronounced sook-ha).

Teacher, doctor, lawyer. These are occupations, but your sukha is much bigger, broader, and more deeply ingrained than any one job title. Helping people grow, aiding in others' health, and standing up for the defenseless. Each of these is an essence.

And yet, from an early age, we are conditioned to skip past essence and go straight to an occupation.

"What do you want to be when you grow up?" is a question we have all been asked, from kindergarten to college. The answer they expected was always a job title. You couldn't say, "I want to boost people's confidence in their appearance." It was, "I want to be a fashion designer or a fitness instructor or an orthodontist."

This carries on into adulthood. "What do you want to be?" turns into "What do you do?" Our identity and our title become intertwined. We become convinced that we *are* our job—and consumed by what *other* people think of it.

In the 1980s, researchers at Dartmouth University devised an experiment. If you were a participant in the study, a professional makeup artist painted a fake "scar" on your face. Imagine a bright-red, lumpy-looking blemish from your right ear down your cheek.

You were then asked to go into a room and have a sit-down conversation with a stranger. Your job was to observe their behavior—how they responded to you and the scar on your face.

But there was a twist. Seconds before you go in, the makeup artist asks if they can give your scar a "touch-up." Instead of touching it up, however, they wipe it off entirely. So you enter the room *believing* you still have a scar on your face.

Later, researchers asked each participant whether the stranger had noticed their scar. Absolutely, they all said. In fact, the stranger couldn't stop staring at it. Some participants claimed that the stranger looked away because the mark was so hideous.

The Dartmouth experiment illuminated a basic human truth: we tend to view ourselves through the eyes of others. We believe *we are* what *they* see. In turn, we make choices that aren't in line with what we want, which leads us farther down a path that doesn't feel like our own.

Like Arjuna, we can easily find ourselves not knowing how to act because we've forgotten who we really are.

The purpose of this book is to bring "who you are" and "how

you act" into harmony. We start by reconnecting you with your essence, your sukha.

"Finding your essence" might seem daunting. But the truth is that your sukha is already inside of you. And as my friend Mila discovered, sometimes all it takes is a simple shift in perspective to see it again.

✦ ✦ ✦

Mila was a project manager at a large software company. She was paid well and could work remotely when she wanted. As a working mom, the position offered her enough flexibility to keep up with family priorities.

But like many of us, Mila felt her job was more of a paycheck than a passion. She was doing good work and helping the company's bottom line, but it was a reach to say any of this excited her.

Externally, she appeared successful. Internally, however, she was languishing.

Elie Wiesel wrote that the opposite of love isn't hate, but indifference. Mila didn't hate her job; she was indifferent to it. And that feeling festered until everything started to seem pointless and drab.

After dropping the kids off at school, Mila always dreaded the next step in her day—opening her laptop and switching her status on Slack from "away" to "active."

Late at night, she would scour job boards, searching for something that might pique her interest. Some of the openings seemed more appealing than her current position, but none felt like a game changer.

She had already switched employers three times in seven years.

Each time she made a move, she hoped it would produce some kind of spark. Even when a new position *did* provide that spark, it never grew into a fire. After a few months, she was back to the same set point, feeling lost and indifferent.

Teaching was the one occupation that captured Mila's imagination. When she closed her eyes, she could see herself looking out at a classroom full of students eager to learn. And she was eager to teach them. The thought of becoming an educator made her come alive.

However, going back to school to get her teaching certificate felt like too much of a stretch. The family depended on Mila's healthcare benefits and salary. Her duties were nonnegotiable and took priority over her dharma.

Then one day, Mila sat down for coffee with her longtime mentor, Denise. Mila had no intention of sharing these feelings. After all, it was her mentor who had helped Mila get to the project management position she was in now.

After a bit of small talk, Denise sensed that something was off. She leaned in, made direct eye contact, and asked her protégé, "How are you *really?*" That's the thing about a great guide—they have a way of piercing the veil and getting to the heart of the matter.

Mila opened up and told her everything. How she was climbing a ladder at work, but moving farther away from what she wanted from life. How teaching was the only thing that really excited her—even though she knew it was never going to happen.

After Mila finished her monologue, Denise sat back in her chair and took a long sip of coffee. Mila braced for impact, expecting to be "set straight." Instead, Denise told Mila how much she admired the part of her that was seeking answers. "So many of us turn away from the deeper questions," she said.

Denise then asked Mila a question that kick-started a journey into her dharma. "What is it *specifically* about teaching that captivates you?"

Mila didn't hesitate with her answer. She admired educators. She loved being around students. She was enamored with the idea of preparing young people for adulthood, just as great teachers had done for her.

Mila paused and looked to Denise for feedback. What she found instead was an arched eyebrow—a face that wanted more.

As Mila sank deeper into the question, she noticed something. A glimmer that felt foreign, yet familiar. Like a long-distance relative whom she adored as a child. For the first time, she was able to go beneath the title of teaching and into the essence that made it so appealing to her.

Full of conviction, Mila said, "I love helping people grow."

In her current job, Mila really enjoyed hiring and helping new people integrate into their roles. She loved investing time in junior project managers, taking them to coffee just like her mentor had done for her.

"Helping people grow" might not seem like an earth-shattering self-discovery. But for Mila, it was an essence, buried underneath years of competing priorities and demands. Even when she *was* helping others grow, she hadn't been aware of it.

After leaving the coffee shop that day, Mila FaceTimed her mom to share her discovery. Watching her daughter's face come alive, Mila's mom smiled with recognition. "Yes, Mila . . . you've been helping people grow since you were two years old."

Mila wiped back tears as she listened to her mom recount stories from her childhood. How as a toddler she took it upon herself to teach her baby cousin how to crawl. How Mila was the first kid in her neighborhood to ride a bike—so she set up a "bicycle camp" for her friends to help them learn.

As Mila got a lucid look at her own essence, a "through line" emerged and the seemingly unrelated dots of her life began to connect.

Nothing had changed, and yet everything had changed.

+ + +

Mila had been fixated on the job title of "teacher." Now she realized that being a teacher was an occupation, not an essence. Her essence was to "help people grow," and expressing that essence didn't require a classroom.

She could become a corporate trainer, a part-time tutor, an executive coach. She could strive for a management role and help the members of her team grow. She could even make a lateral shift to HR and focus on nurturing other people's careers.

Suddenly, Mila began to breathe more easily. It was as if she had been in a pressure cooker, relentlessly trying to find her "one thing," and someone had lifted the release valve. For the first time since college, she felt open to the possibilities of the world.

With a clearer sense of her own sukha, Mila began reaching out to colleagues for ideas on how to express it. Most of them didn't have any leads, but each conversation helped her crystallize her own thinking. She had been through job searches before, but this one felt different. This time around, she was enjoying herself. When you know your essence, the search for an expression is part of the fun.

Eventually, one of Mila's coworkers came to her with an opportunity. Their department was launching a new leadership program. Twenty recruits would rotate through key areas of the company, exposing them to new people and ideas. The program was looking for a coordinator to recruit the talent, build their curriculum, and connect them with mentors inside the company.

Mila immediately threw her hat in the ring and got the job.

Over the next three years, she scaled the program internationally. She became an active speaker at universities and a go-to mentor for young leaders. Not a workday went by when she didn't, in some small way, help other people grow.

It was the most lit up Mila had ever felt in her career.

The beauty of it all is that she didn't have to make wholesale changes in her life. She didn't have to switch industries or go back to school. She didn't even have to leave her company.

Did Mila believe that this was the final stop on her path? No. Everything would continue to change. Her family's needs, the world of work, and even her own personal interests.

But now that she understood her essence, she would always know who she was and how to act.

THE FOUR CHISELS

It's easy to recognize when you're lost in the woods. The hard part is finding your way home.

After selling my healthcare company, RISE, Bauji's words and wisdom were back in my head. I knew I had to find my way back to the center of the wheel, I just didn't know how.

Discovering my dharma felt like an overwhelming task. I was

afraid I would invest a lot of time and energy trying to "find my-self" and end up more lost than ever before.

But Mila's story made me realize something: Dharma is *not* a destination. It isn't something you need to go looking for, because it's been with you since the day you were born and will *never* leave your side.

Michelangelo would look at a block of marble and say the sculpture is already inside. He only had to chisel away at what wasn't necessary.

The same is true for your dharma. You don't need to *find* it; you just have to remove the layers that are in its way. That means chipping away at everything that has buried your essence—including other people's priorities, expectations, and judgments.

There are four different chisels I've found most useful in getting to your core. Four tools to help you uncover your essence and show you new ways to express it.

As you start to chisel away, be aware of what immediately comes up, and also honor the part of you that wants to take its time. Certain insights may arise right away, while others will unfold over the course of our journey together. Sometimes, you chisel a bit and find nothing notable. Then days or even weeks later, layers unexpectedly crumble to the ground.

#1: THE BRIGHT SPOTS CHISEL

Anthony de Mello, an Indian Jesuit priest and psychotherapist, would tell his audiences there is only one reason you're not experiencing joy at this moment: because you're focused on what you *don't* have.

When we aren't satisfied with our work, there is a tendency to feel like *everything* about it is wrong. We focus almost entirely on what feels off and dismiss what feels right.

That's not to say that we should suck it up and stay in jobs that make us miserable. Quite the opposite. We can use the moments that cause us misery to better understand what brings us joy.

We do that by identifying the "bright spots." These are tiny diamonds in the rough of otherwise difficult times and circumstances. To find them, ask yourself a simple question: Even if you hate your job right now, are there any moments that bring you joy?

My days as a tech entrepreneur and CEO—while far from my dharma—were also not completely unhappy. There were bright spots, and it didn't take me long to recall them.

The first thing that came to mind was pitching RISE to potential investors. For a long stretch, my days were just one presentation after another. I know a lot of people find this stressful, but I was enjoying getting up in front of groups.

I remembered one meeting in particular. The investors seemed disinterested, checking their watches and phones while I spoke. My first instinct was to cut my losses, quickly wrap things up, and move on with my day. Instead, I decided to try something different.

I told them my story.

When I was a kid and my dad was in his midforties, he was overweight and in poor health. One day, we had to rush him to the hospital for emergency open-heart surgery. I described to these investors how I nearly lost my dad that day, and how his life has never been the same.

Inside that boardroom, I experienced every emotion I felt at eleven years old, standing next to Dad's hospital bed. Finally, I snapped back into the room and realized those investors were now totally engrossed. Moments later, they agreed to become my first backers.

That day, I realized the power of a personal, heartfelt story. What it meant for others, and what it meant to me.

The more I looked back on my years as an entrepreneur, the more I realized something. Every moment I truly enjoyed— whether it was pitching investors, listening to customers, or motivating my team—involved a story. Every bright spot involved me receiving or sharing a narrative.

When I chiseled away the layers and took a deeper look at myself, I was able to see that my essence is to *tell stories*. At my core, I'm a storyteller. And that's more important, more meaningful, than any job title or occupation.

By pinpointing the bright spots of a job I *didn't like*, I was able to reconnect with something that I truly loved. And with this chisel in your tool belt, you can always turn a difficult experience into the starting point for your dharma.

#2: THE POSSIBILITY CHISEL

Once you're connected to your essence, ideas for how to express it will unfold naturally.

Your sukha, by its nature, is dynamic, expansive, and playful. There are *lots* of ways that it wants to engage with the world. When you begin to reconnect with your essence, don't be surprised if it suddenly unleashes a fountain spring of options.

When I realized my essence was telling stories, I immediately began to reminisce about my former life as a speechwriter. It became obvious that the reason I loved writing speeches so much is because it was a form of storytelling.

Instead of pinning my dharma to the past, however, I started brainstorming ways that storytelling could be part of my future. I could start a podcast, give speeches, teach a class, write books, make films.

When options pop into your head, try to avoid becoming attached to one right away. Instead, open up to the possibilities. Because when you broaden yourself to new ways of expressing your essence, you'll start to see inspiration everywhere you look.

You might spot a character in a film who has a unique job. You might meet someone at a cocktail party who is working on a fascinating project. You might see a volunteer role in a local organization that really lights you up.

One of the greatest places to find inspiration is inside a *magazine aisle*. It might sound strange, but a walk down a well-stocked lane of magazines is like taking a trip into the collective dharma of our planet. It's an explosion of tastes, interests, and expressions.

There are publications dedicated to cooking, cats, crochet, and cranes. Lighthouses, goats, bridges, and whiskey. There is the *OMFG (official meeting facilities guide)* magazine, *Modern Drunkard Magazine*, and *Spudman* magazine: "the most trusted voice in the potato industry."

I find this liberating. They are unapologetically expressing their essence, and that inspires me to express mine.

Give the "magazine walk" a try. Find an aisle inside a library, bookstore, or airport boutique. Slowly walk from one side to the other and pick up any publications that capture your interest.

Bring awareness to *why* each magazine is pulling you in. And don't be afraid to leave your comfort zone and explore a new area that interests you—even if your friends would find it boring. This is a chance to wipe away the scar and see the world with your *own* eyes.

When I began taking magazine walks, I was surprised to find that the publications I was most drawn to were all focused on spirituality. I would read and re-read articles by people who were bringing ancient insights to modern times. Authors, teachers, and poets—from Ram Dass to Maria Popova to Ryan Holiday.

I buried myself in their work. Each trip to the library felt like a return to Bauji's porch. Each story felt like a piece of his wisdom.

My essence was coming alive, and I was now considering a new way of expressing it. What if I could tap into the lessons of dharma that my grandfather taught me many years ago? And what if I could somehow share those practices with the world?

#3: THE DHARMA DECK CHISEL

Bauji would say that you can do anything—but you can't do everything.

To make our mark, we have to stay open to possibilities, and also *prioritize* what we're seeing. At some point, we have to choose an expression so that we can give it the energy it deserves.

Opening up and prioritizing at the same time can be tricky. One tool to help is what I call a "dharma deck." Here's how it works:

Each time you find an expression that inspires you, write it down on the front of an index card. Mila, for example, would have a separate card for teacher, HR professional, corporate trainer, and tutor—all different expressions that tapped into her essence of helping people grow.

On the back of each card, describe what it is about this position that excites you. Go beneath the title, the status, the salary—and get specific about what you find captivating.

Fairly quickly, you'll begin to assemble your dharma deck. Every week or so, set aside a few quiet moments to sort the cards from top to bottom. The expressions that are captivating you the most go to the top of the pile.

What you might notice is that week after week a couple of cards retain their position at the top of the pack. Pay special attention to these. Everything in the deck is worth your attention but the ones at the top are calling out to you the most.

During a magazine walk, I came across an author named Stephen Cope, who wrote about the Bhagavad Gita. At first, I was a bit skeptical of a white man from the Midwest writing about this sacred Indian text.

But after devouring *The Great Work of Your Life* by Cope, my entire worldview changed. He had brought Eastern wisdom to a Western audience through practical lessons and beautifully told stories. After finishing the last chapter, I created an index card that said "Write a book that follows in Cope's footsteps."

Week after week, that card remained at the top of my dharma deck. I realized that there was nothing I'd rather do with my time—no other expression that my essence wanted more.

It would take me several years to turn that idea into a reality. And as you'll see in future chapters, the path was windy and full of setbacks. But all of it brought us to the book you're holding and the journey we're on together now.

#4: THE PICASSO CHISEL

There's a quote I love that is often credited to Pablo Picasso: "The meaning of life is to find your gift; the purpose of life is to give it away."

That's not to say you need to work for free, but rather to recognize that money can muddy the waters of dharma. Whenever you're considering a new job or project, try to channel Picasso's wisdom and ask: Would I do it for free? If the answer is yes, that means the role is almost certainly a way for you to express your essence.

A few months ago, a close friend asked me to give his son some career advice. Levi was a junior in college, and when we jumped on our video chat, he dove right into his ambitions for after graduation.

Levi told me he wanted to work as a financial analyst with a top firm in Chicago. He told me it was a highly competitive role, and that many of his friends who graduated last year weren't selected. Levi had his hopes set on this specific job and was clearly anxious that he might not get it.

I asked him to tell me more about his goal to be a financial analyst. What was so appealing to him about that role? Levi's answers came quickly. He told me he loved building budgets and financial models from scratch. He enjoyed creating tools that others could use. To him, spreadsheets were more than just rows and columns—they were living, breathing tools that could help people make critical decisions.

Levi then shared that, since his freshman year, he had been volunteering at the small-business clinic on campus. The clinic offered free financial advice to local entrepreneurs. Levi was now devoting ten to fifteen hours each week to the clinic.

I asked him why. If he was looking for a résumé-builder, he could volunteer a fraction of that time and still get the credit. What was driving him to commit so much of his schedule each week to local business owners?

That's when Levi told me about his uncle Jim.

Uncle Jim owned a small bakery in their neighborhood outside of Chicago. He was wonderful with people and he loved to bake. But his least favorite part of the job was leaving the front counter to go into his tiny back office and work on "the books." As a result, he neglected key financial commitments and eventually found himself in too much debt to keep his business alive. The bakery went bankrupt.

Uncle Jim was never the same. He became depressed and angry, someone that Levi no longer recognized. As a kid, Levi would wake up on Saturday mornings to the smells and sounds of Uncle Jim cooking his famous chocolate chip pancakes and belting out Bob Seger songs. He brought life and energy to every room he was in. And he made Levi happy.

But Levi hadn't seen his uncle in years. No one had.

Through the screen, Levi's eyes turned red and puffy. Then he looked at me through his camera. "I could have helped him," he said.

I wouldn't have predicted that a conversation about spreadsheets would end so emotionally. But that's what happens when you go beneath a title and understand its essence. When you get to why it *really* matters to you.

Levi had a career goal to be a financial analyst at a top firm. But underneath that occupation was a strong dharmic pull to help people like his uncle Jim make life-changing financial decisions.

Being an analyst was one way Levi could express that essence. But there were clearly others.

We began to brainstorm alternatives. He could join the clinic full-time. He could become a CPA serving small businesses. He could join an incubator that trained aspiring entrepreneurs. He and his classmates could create a Finance 101 master class for brick-and-mortar shops.

As we rattled off options, a heavy weight seemed to lift from Levi's shoulders. He still wanted that analyst role in Chicago, but his horizons were expanding. He no longer believed that a yes-or-no decision from a hiring manager could keep him from expressing his essence.

By better understanding what Levi would do for free, and why, we quickly chiseled to the core of who he is, and ways he could share that with the world. It's a simple and wonderful tactic that I wish I knew earlier in my life—and one that you can put into practice no matter where you are in your career.

♦ ♦ ♦

Your essence, your sukha, never leaves you—though the way you express it can change over time. I watched my dad learn this during a painful period in his life. After thirty years in the automotive industry, both he and my mom lost their jobs.

It was the early 2000s and the economy was melting down in Detroit. On the same day, my parents were both given pink slips. They walked out of their building together, holding hands, never to return.

I didn't worry about my mom because she had so many other

interests. She started a garden, experimented with new styles of cooking, and spent a lot more time with my grandmother.

Dad was a different story. Being an engineer was the only way he knew how to express his essence. He was a builder at heart and he loved putting things together. Without his job, he really didn't know what to do with himself.

On the first day of his forced retirement, he found his way to the living room recliner and didn't get up. We worried about his heart condition and his mental health. We would plead with him to find something, anything, to occupy his time. He resisted, flipping back and forth between sitcom reruns and market updates.

A couple of months later, I decided to surprise my parents with a drop-in visit from college. It was a Friday evening, and when I arrived I was startled to see two police officers standing at my front door.

They were speaking to my dad, who looked like a new man. He was freshly shaven and wearing a crisp, clean-looking dress shirt. And while these cops were clearly not pleased, Dad was smiling.

"Just keep the noise down, okay?" one of the officers said before turning away. Confused, I entered the house, following my dad's lead into a room packed full of people. Some of them were faces I recognized—aunts, uncles, and family friends. Others were complete strangers; all of them were well into their late fifties and sixties. One guy was strumming a sitar, while a woman nearby rocked from side to side like she was watching Ravi Shankar at Woodstock.

As my dad entered the room, they all snickered and looked to him for a report. Dad took a big swig from his glass of scotch, then shouted, "They said we're being too loud!" The room erupted in delight.

That's when Dad walked over to a machine with a mic plugged into the side. Next to it was a notebook that he picked up and examined. A mischievous smile came over his face, then he turned to the crowd and shouted, "Mukesh's turn!"

It turns out that when Dad was lying in his recliner, his mind wasn't just glued to the television. It had wandered to his childhood in India. To the local cinema where he and his friends would catch the newly released Raj Kapoor films. To the rickshaw rides home, caroling the soundtracks he already knew by heart, arms flailing out the sides of the vehicle. These were periods of true joy that my father had all but forgotten.

Then one day on CNBC he heard that you could find *any* song ever made on Napster. That led to Dad ripping his childhood favorites onto a CD. Which led to him buying a discount karaoke machine from Costco. Which eventually led to him inviting friends over to show off his new discovery.

In the months that followed, those friends grew into a rapidly expanding karaoke group. Every Friday became a standing-room-only Bollywood bash at the Guptas' three-bedroom home in metro Detroit.

Over time, I began to realize how important those parties were to my dad, and to the others inside that room. The economy in Michigan had only gotten tougher, and many of those people had also lost their jobs. To them, karaoke wasn't just something to do on a Friday night; it provided a sense of purpose throughout the week.

On Monday, you were choosing your song. By Wednesday you had committed it to memory. By Thursday, you were selecting your outfit and preparing an aromatic dish to bring to the party. By the time karaoke night arrived, you'd incorporated a dance routine that was sure to outdo the others. This wasn't just a get-together; it was a talent show.

As for Dad, karaoke wasn't just about singing—it was a return to his essence. Engineer and karaoke coordinator were entirely different jobs. And yet, beneath the titles, there was a surprising overlap.

Both roles allowed him to build, assemble, and bring things together. Before each karaoke gathering, he was hardwiring microphone splitters, collating playlists, and pushing Napster's feature set to its limits.

Karaoke allowed Dad to express the very same essence he had channeled as an automotive engineer—only with more freedom and creativity than he ever found inside a cubicle.

Growing up, I rarely saw my dad get excited about guests arriving at the house. Now he'd rip open the door and shake people's hands like he was angling for their vote.

As the years passed, and the members of the group got older, the community he built grew even closer. When a fellow singer reached the end of her life, I watched Dad and his friends surround her hospital bed and tenderly harmonize a tune that she had once performed inside my living room.

When COVID-19 shuttered everyone into isolation, Dad transitioned the community to Zoom, supplying people with a sense of joy that would have otherwise felt impossible.

Dad's story is proof that we are more than our job titles. That our essence runs deeper than any single occupation. I never once saw Dad introduce himself to others as a karaoke coordinator. He didn't have a LinkedIn profile and never received a salary.

But it was clear to me—and everyone around him—that he was living his dharma.

CHAPTER TWO

BHAKTI

FULL-HEARTED DEVOTION

In *The Alchemist*, Paulo Coelho shares a story about a young shopkeeper seeking the secret to happiness. The boy travels forty days by foot to the castle of the wisest man in the world. When he finally reaches the palace, the wise man agrees to share the secret—but only after the boy explores the castle.

The boy agrees, but before he sets out, the wise man hands him a teaspoon carrying two drops of oil. "As you wander around, carry this spoon with you without allowing the oil to spill."

The boy walks around the palace completely fixated on the spoon. He returns after a couple of hours, proudly showing the wise man that the drops of oil haven't spilled.

The wise man asks, "Did you see the Persian tapestries that are hanging in my dining hall? Did you see the garden that took the master gardener ten years to create? Did you notice the beautiful parchments in my library?"

The embarrassed boy admits that he hadn't seen any of those

things. He was too fixated on the spoon. "Then go back and observe the marvels of my world," the wise man insists.

So the young shopkeeper sets out again, and this time he notices everything—the lovely gardens, the blooming flowers, the majestic mountains. He returns with awe, recounting all the beauty he'd seen.

"But where are the drops of oil I entrusted to you?" asks the wise man. The boy looks down to find that the spoon is empty.

"Well, there is only one piece of advice I can give you," says the wisest of wise men. "The secret of happiness is to see all the marvels of the world, and never to forget the drops of oil on the spoon."

The drops of oil in this story are our duties, while the surrounding beauty is our dharma.

The duties we face can seem so immediate and urgent that they absorb all our focus. Even when we are clear on our dharma, we don't always have the time to invest in it.

Duties and dharma can often seem like archenemies, as if one is always trying to squeeze out the other. And because duties are often nonnegotiable, our dharma is usually the one to get cut when the schedule is tight.

Bhakti (pronounced bach-tee) is the practice of "full-hearted devotion." You can think of bhakti as the opposite of distraction. While distractions take us away from our dharma, bhakti brings us closer.

And yet bhakti is less about the devotion of time, and more about the devotion of heart. We tend to focus too much on the number of hours we bring to a task—and not enough on the quality we bring to each hour.

Monks, for example, are deeply devoted to the practice of meditation. But they don't meditate around the clock. Their days are also dedicated to duties—working the land, maintaining the monastery, and preparing meals.

The illusion we sometimes have is that extraordinary people spend their days entirely focused on their purpose. Not true. In fact, many of the world's greatest thinkers worked full-time jobs.

Poet T. S. Eliot was a banker.

Artist Richard Serra delivered furniture.

Novelist Kurt Vonnegut was a car salesman.

Writer and artist Henry Darger was a janitor.

There's a story I love about Philip Glass, the great American composer who was also a plumber. One day, Glass was installing a dishwasher inside a posh apartment in New York's SoHo neighborhood. He was kneeling on the floor with dish racks and pump parts surrounding him when he heard an audible gasp.

The owner of the apartment was Robert Hughes, an art critic for *TIME* magazine, who was staring at Glass in disbelief. "You're Philip Glass. What are you doing here?"

"I'm installing your dishwasher," Glass replied.

"But you're an artist," protested the critic.

"I *am* an artist," Glass shot back. "And I'm sometimes a plumber as well, so you should go away and let me finish."

Bhakti teaches us that there is a difference between being fully scheduled and full-hearted. When it comes to your dharma, it's much better to be full-hearted and partly scheduled than fully scheduled and half-hearted.

We're about to go deeper into the difference so that you no longer see duty and dharma as enemies, but allies. When those two are aligned, duty fuels your dharma and dharma fuels your duties.

DHARMA VS. DUTIES

As a single working mother of two boys, Toni Morrison's duties seemed endless. Her job as a book editor came with one meeting or deadline after another. Her job as a mom required her to shuttle the kids to school, appointments, and practices before coming home to make meals, help with homework, do the housework, and get the kids to bed on time.

One night, after the boys were asleep, Morrison sat down and created a list of everything she still needed to get done. After finishing, she tried to stand up from the table, but couldn't. Her legs simply refused to move.

Staring at that piece of paper, Morrison was paralyzed by a realization. She had long dreamed of becoming an author, and yet "writing" was nowhere to be found on her extensive to-do list. She was stuck in the shadow of her own dharma: editing other people's books instead of writing one herself.

Each year seemed to pass more quickly than the one before it, and in the midst of so many duties, her dreams were slipping away.

Morrison slowly reached her hand across the desk and pulled out a fresh piece of paper. Then she closed her eyes and asked herself a profound question: What are the things that if I *don't* do . . . I will die inside?

Only two items made the cut: "Mother my children" and "Write books." One represented her deepest duty, and the other her deepest sense of dharma.

The other commitments on her to-do list hadn't vanished, but she now felt a renewed sense of clarity. She knew what was most important and, therefore, where her devotion must lie. It was time to stop playing the Game of Someday and start playing the Game of Now.

The very next morning, Morrison began a new routine that would continue throughout her life and career. She woke up at five a.m. to rise "before the light arrived." This was less an act of time management, and more an act of bhakti.

Her mornings were typically chaotic and filled with duties. Now she had transformed them into a sacred space for her dharma.

Morrison would wrap her hands around a warm mug of coffee and watch the sunrise. Then she would write until her kids woke up. It was in those early hours, between the last sip of coffee and the first utterance of "Mama," that she began to fill her pages.

When the day's duties began, her dharma stuck with her. Suddenly ordinary events—dropping her kids off at school, riding the bus to work, and meetings with colleagues—became moments of inspiration for her writing. She would jot ideas, events, and stories down on little scraps of paper.

Then the following morning, after sipping on her warm beverage and watching the dawn sky, she would turn those tiny scraps into paragraphs and pages, eventually into chapters and books.

Toni Morrison was the first African American woman to win the Nobel Prize for literature. And she didn't start writing until she was in her thirties, as a single working mother of two. Her duties hadn't changed, and her commitments remained the same.

What changed was her devotion.

Poet Johann Wolfgang von Goethe said that "at the moment of commitment the entire universe conspires to assist you." Morrison found that committing to her dharma didn't require her to put in forty hours a week, but rather every bit of her being. She had to remain connected to it each day, even when she was tied up with other things.

RITUAL: TURN DISTRACTIONS INTO INSPIRATION

Life is full of distractions, but when you're tuning in the right way, those interruptions can spark our imagination.

We often get hit with inspiration when we least expect it. Researcher Michael Gelb surveyed thousands of people on where they come up with their best ideas. Some of the most common answers were: while taking a shower, resting in bed, walking in nature, and listening to music.

You know what almost no one answered? "While sitting at my desk."

When inspiration hits, you may not be able to drop everything you're doing, but the key is to make sure you capture it. This is why Toni Morrison was constantly jotting things down on scraps of paper—no matter where she was. By doing so, she ensured that no good idea was ever lost. So make sure you always have a way to record inspiration whenever or wherever it hits.

I like to carry around a 3.5″ x 5.5″ notebook. It's plain-looking on the outside, lined on the inside, and fits in my back pocket. I call it my "dharma notes."

Each time I have a thought related to my dharma, I pull out my notebook and write it down. I try not to use my phone for dharma notes, because the second I look at my screen and spot a notification, I get swept away by something else. I lose the moment.

How you record your thoughts is less important. What matters is getting into the habit of capturing what excites you. Even the tiniest details. The pitch of a stranger's voice, the aromas inside a coffee shop, the font on a street sign. This practice will train your senses to spot inspiration inside seemingly ordinary moments. And when that happens, you'll start to feel like everything that surrounds you is somehow related to your dharma. Because it is.

DUTIES FUEL YOUR DHARMA

Marshall Mathers and Berry Gordy both launched their careers inside cluttered, noisy automotive factories in Detroit. They both knew that their dharma was making music, not machines. But neither had the savings to turn their dharma into a full-time career. Yet these two musical icons didn't dismiss their day jobs as wasteful. Instead, they found a way to take in the setting around them without dropping the oil on the spoon.

Mathers, aka Eminem, tuned in to the motions of the factory—the tearing of scrap metal, the punch of the press machines. On his bus ride home, he absorbed the raw scenery of 8 Mile Road, cultivating these images into lyrics that he married to the sounds of steel from the plant.

Berry Gordy worked the assembly line at Ford Motor Company to make ends meet. It wasn't the job he would have chosen, but like Eminem, he used his duties to inspire his dharma.

Through the assembly line, Gordy observed a hunk of metal transform into a fully finished vehicle. He began to believe he could do the same for musicians—create a "sound factory" that turned unproven musical talent into singing sensations.

Gordy began to carefully study the specifics of the assembly line. How was it organized? Who ensured the quality? What happened when something needed a redo?

Then, in his spare time, Gordy began to build Motown Records, a new kind of music studio that closely resembled what he observed at that Ford plant. Instead of flooring, chassis, and engines, it was voicework, wardrobe, and media training.

New artists would enter Gordy's studio with little more than raw talent, and they would exit as polished stars. Stevie Wonder, Diana Ross, Marvin Gaye, Gladys Knight, and Smokey Robinson were among the greats who went through Gordy's assembly line and collectively created the sound of Motown.

If given the choice, do you think Eminem or Berry Gordy would have decided to work inside a factory? Probably not.

But they didn't let that time go to waste either. They let their duties fuel their dharma, drawing inspiration from the imagery and imagination around them.

RITUAL: EMBODYING YOUR DHARMA

When you're drowning in duties, it's easy to disconnect from your dharma. We have to find ways to keep reminding ourselves of who we are. Remember when Philip Glass was installing a dishwasher, he exclaimed "I *am* an artist."

This is the exact kind of daily reinforcement we need to give ourselves. And one of the most effective ways to keep that connection is to "wear it." To literally keep a reminder of your dharma somewhere on your physical body.

I have a piece of paper inside my pocket that says "I am a storyteller." I need the reminder because sometimes I get so overwhelmed by duties and distractions that I completely forget about my essence.

It might sound strange or simplistic, but that little piece of paper always brings me back to center. I might not be doing anything related to telling stories at that moment, but I still feel connected to my dharma.

Give it a try: Write down something that you feel describes your essence, and carry it around with you. If you're an accountant who writes poetry, for example, that piece of paper will keep you connected to your poet-self, even during tax season.

From time to time, reach down and trace your fingers over your piece of paper. Feel the words permeate through your fingertips.

DHARMA FUELS YOUR DUTIES

Karen Struck grew up about an hour north of Boston. During her junior year at Haverhill High School she was told by her English teacher, Ms. LeGendre, that she had a gift for writing. Karen took this observation to heart and pursued the written word with vigor for the rest of high school, writing for the school paper and even publishing op-eds in the local newspaper.

After graduating with the class of 1972, her college required her to declare a major. That piece of paper represented a fork in the road: Should she pursue arts or analytics?

For Ms. LeGendre, Karen's decision should have been clear cut. Her student was uniquely gifted with the written word, and it would be a shame if that talent wasn't developed. But Karen's parents felt differently. To them, writing was a hobby, not a career.

So Karen sharpened a no. 2 pencil and circled: "Nursing."

Skillwise, being a nurse turned out to be a good fit for Karen. She was naturally warm, attentive, and responsive. Before long, she was promoted to lead nurse of the intensive care unit.

When you're not on the path of your own dharma, a promotion can seem bittersweet. It can feel like both an advancement and a departure.

In hospitals, one of the major downsides of taking a leadership role is the paperwork. You're filling out lots of forms, detailing the background of each patient.

Most hospital workers view this task as a massive burden. But Karen came to enjoy writing these reports. To her, a medical record didn't just represent a patient's history, but their story—how they made a living, how they spent their evenings, and who was in their life.

And while most nurses would quickly type out the essential overview and hit print, Karen took her time. Inside the break room, with the faint scent of antiseptic seeping in, Karen would type to the hum of a vending machine. In these moments, she would often think of Ms. LeGendre, the one person who told her that writing really could be her life's work.

As Karen expressed her essence, she felt a spark flicker again. The gates that had isolated her dharma for so many years were beginning to open, and everyone around her noticed.

Karen's coworkers eagerly waited for her reports, which not only contained the pertinent medical facts, but flowed with the rhythm and nuance of a novel. Every once in a while, a doctor or a nurse would pull Karen aside, overcome with emotion. Her reports were connecting them back to the humanity of their work. Each of her stories was a reminder of their own dharma, a reminder of why they had gone into medicine in the first place.

By bringing her writing to the hospital, she had taken her dharma into her duties. Now, a voice inside her head was telling her to take her duties into her dharma.

Karen started writing screenplays about the families she had observed and supported inside the Emergency Room. The first plot in Karen's mind was based on a story she'd seen up close. A twelve-year-old girl's mom dies suddenly, and after the funeral, her father completely shuts down. Her grandfather takes on the role of caretaker, but after nearly dying from a heart attack himself, he has no choice but to teach his own son how to be a father.

Karen's dream was to have her script picked up by a major studio, securing her spot as a backable Hollywood screenwriter.

That didn't happen. Oftentimes, the doorway back to our dharma opens to a path, not a peak. Some of us take a look, realize it's not the top, and shut the door altogether. But Karen decided to keep on walking.

She spent the next eight years pitching her screenplays and ideas to anyone in the film industry who would listen. During that period, she was turned down by 187 different agents. One year of rejection is tough. Three years is heartbreaking. Eight years is agony. Meanwhile, she had entered her fifties, and friends were telling her: "You gave it a shot . . . now it's time to move on."

It was bhakti—full-hearted devotion—that kept Karen going.

Without nursing, Karen couldn't make a living. Without writing, she couldn't live. So she continued on.

Then, after nearly a decade of devotion, and with little to lose, she reached out to Tom Wertheimer, a former patient whom she connected with while he was under her care. Tom was an executive at Universal. He read her script, and it moved him to tears. With Tom signed on as a producer, Karen's screenplay was made into a TV movie, *Charlie & Me*.

Most successful screenwriters break into the industry in their twenties or thirties. Karen received her first break at the age of fifty-two. After that, she became known around Hollywood as the nurse-turned-writer. Karen's experience allowed her to capture the patient experience on paper and with authenticity. Within a few years, she was leading writing rooms for Emmy Award–winning medical dramas like *The Good Doctor* and *The Night Shift*.

Karen Struck is a reminder that dharma doesn't require a return to the past. It can be a permutation of the present.

She became a symbol of possibility and perseverance to people around Los Angeles as well as to folks in her tiny hometown of Haverhill, Massachusetts. Shortly after her first film was released, the local paper did a story on their hometown hero's unlikely journey.

The morning the article was published, Ms. LeGendre, Karen's now-retired English teacher, received a phone call. It was the hospital asking her to come in immediately for a follow-up with the doctor. During that conversation, Ms. LeGendre was diagnosed with lung cancer.

On the ride home from the hospital, Ms. LeGendre began to ask the questions that you and I might both ask when we're near the end. *What difference did I make in the world? Who did I help? How did I matter?*

When she got home, she noticed an opened copy of the *Haverhill Gazette*. She had not seen Karen in over thirty years but instantly recognized her face. Ms. LeGendre held the paper in her hands and traced her fingers with pride over her former student's photo. Then she read the first lines of the article.

When Karen Struck was a junior at Haverhill High School in 1971, she fell in love with the written word thanks to English teacher Marilyn LeGendre.

Sometimes duty is a call to action. A call to serve, to care, to love. And sometimes if you look hard enough, duty is simply a reminder of the dharma you've been living all along.

RITUAL: WANDERING TIME

One of the greatest gifts you can give your dharma is "wandering time." This is a time when you get to just be with your craft, rather than aiming to achieve something.

Roam free, contemplate, and dream without any pressure to produce an outcome. Wandering time is intentionally *non*productive.

The neuroscience is very clear on how important this is for your dharma. Quiet, disconnected periods are scientifically proven to boost creative thinking and near-term productivity. Dr. Teresa Belton from the UK studies the interconnection between boredom and imagination. Through her in-depth studies of highly successful people, Belton has found boredom to be a critical source of creative inspiration. This is why many child psychologists recommend that we let our children be bored during summer vacations, rather than jam-packing their calendars with activities.

We've been conditioned to remove blank slots in our schedule and pack them with productivity. The sentiment is that if we're not doing something, then we're not doing enough.

And yet some of the most profound *doers* were serious about building wandering time into their schedules. Steve Jobs, for example, was known to take long, meandering walks to noodle on new ideas.

Albert Einstein was a sailor. He named his boat *Tinef*, which means "trash" in Yiddish. Sailing off the coast of Long Island, Einstein would often get so lost in thought that he'd lose his bearings. Locals said they observed a "strange man who seemed lost at sea."

Sometimes Einstein would dock his boat at the first location he could find and walk around to continue his brainstorming. One time he was apparently so absorbed in thought that he was stopped by the Long Island police officers who assumed Einstein was lost. And yet Einstein credits these aimless expeditions with his most breakthrough thinking.

So every couple of weeks, schedule a date with your dharma. Take it for a long walk. Go on an adventure, however brief. Have a silent meal. During this time, don't listen to a podcast or anything else that will introduce new thoughts. Don't pack those slots with productive activities. Sometimes, your dharma doesn't need productivity, but presence.

◆ ◆ ◆

My friend Rich moved into our suburb in Michigan during my freshman year of high school. I'd later learn that he hadn't moved to Michigan as much as fled to Michigan. Rich's dad died when he was only ten years old. The man his mother married next was physically abusive to both her and Rich. One night, the two got in a car and drove off in search of a new home. They ended up a couple of miles away from me.

Rich and I connected immediately. He was the new kid, I was the brown kid.

We started hanging out, playing video games and basketball. We discussed the girls we liked, prodding and pushing each other to do something about it, knowing with certainty that neither of us ever would. And we bonded over our tough-as-nails moms.

One day after school, as Rich grabbed something from his bedroom, I took a peek inside. What I saw floored me.

There were watercolor paintings hung on every square inch of his wall. They were stunning. Alluring mosaics, deep colors, and intricate details. Each contained emotion—sadness, hurt, hope.

Rich and I had spent a lot of time together, but I had no clue he was even interested in art. He had hidden it from me and everyone else at school. But from what I saw that day, it was clear that painting was more than a hobby, it was his obsession.

Over the next few years, Rich slowly started to bring his art into the open. In college, it became a part of who he was. He'd walk across campus carrying a fold-up easel everywhere he went. To pay his tuition, he worked in construction. Sometimes he'd be inspired by the way the light hit the equipment, so he'd spend his lunch painting what he saw, turning ordinary moments into works of art.

A couple of years after college, Rich told me that he'd been accepted into a prestigious apprenticeship program in Florence,

Italy. He'd be leaving the country to build his life as a full-time painter.

I look back on that conversation as one of my first brushes with dharma, an up-close observation of someone taking a big risk in order to express their essence.

Rich flourished in Italy. He woke each morning to the smell of fresh bread and sounds of the language of love spoken on the streets below. He made art throughout the day and showcased his paintings in the evenings in beautifully lit piazzas.

Then one day, he received a phone call that turned his entire world upside down. Rich's mom, the person he loved more than anyone else, was in a coma. She had gone to the hospital for a minor procedure, but during the operation, her body went into septic shock.

One out of every three patients who suffer through this do not survive. Rich's mom eventually woke up from her coma, but she was never the same. She was going to be dependent on someone else for the rest of her life.

For Rich, there was no question that he would be that person.

He moved back to Michigan to be close to her. One of his first steps was to take a job at Trader Joe's to help pay their bills. Just like that, Rich's life had shifted from mingling with global artisans and painting in piazzas to unloading freight trucks and stocking shelves.

Through it all, Rich never stopped painting, and he never stopped viewing himself as an artist. Just as he did when working construction, he'd observe the tiniest details. The exhaust from a delivery truck escaping into cold Michigan air. The excitement on a young customer's face when they saw the store's holiday treats return for the season. Rich absorbed it all through the prism of art, jotting details into his notebook that he could relish later in front of his easel. His duties began to fuel his dharma. And over time, his dharma also began to fuel his duties.

While visiting another Trader Joe's location, Rich noticed a lack of decor on the walls. This store was new and in a less-populated area of Michigan, so Rich took it upon himself to paint them a mural.

Bringing dharma to duty, he created a beautiful mash-up of iconic images and figures from the area that filled the locals with pride. The painting was a hit, and Rich started receiving calls from other locations asking for the same, this time for a fee.

As Rich's work flourished, he started to see his dream more clearly. How he could finally earn a living from his dharma. He'd open an atelier and teach a new generation of artists. He put together a plan and started to save every extra dollar for a lease on studio space.

While Rich was getting closer to executing his plan, his mom's health was further deteriorating. She had lost most of her mobility and needed to be in a place that was fully equipped with wheelchair accessibility. Rich knew his mom despised the idea of being in a nursing home. Years before, he had promised to help her avoid that fate.

So Rich put all the money he'd saved into buying a house for himself and his mother, a place where she could be comfortable. Becoming his mom's caretaker, in addition to his job at Trader Joe's, left very little time or money for the studio he longed to build.

After years of fighting for his dharma and getting so close to it, the realities of life had become so overbearing that Rich could feel it slipping away.

In this moment of doubt, Rich began to channel the spirit of bhakti. He knew in his heart that time and money were not as important as devotion.

He brainstormed ways to keep his dream alive. That's when it hit him: he could convert his garage into an atelier. It'd be far less costly than a lease, and he'd be nearby whenever his mom needed him.

So for two years, every spare minute Rich had went into converting the space into a proper studio, until he was finally ready to open the *Detroit Atelier.* While I was in the middle of writing this book, Rich invited me to attend a party to commemorate the occasion.

When I walked into the studio, I felt immediately transported back to high school, to the time I poked my head inside Rich's bedroom and saw stunning works of art hanging on his walls. Surrounding Rich was a group of students and artists. Some would be enrolling in the school, others helped build it or inspired him along the way. Meanwhile, Rich's mom was beaming with pride as she stood by the door, welcoming guests.

It was an almost surreal scene for me. Here I was, writing a book about dharma, watching one of my best friends truly live his.

Rich noticed me from the corner of the room, came over, and gave me a *How about this?* sort of look. I gave him a hug and told him how happy I was for him. But at that moment, I struggled to articulate everything I wanted to say.

So I'll say it now.

Rich, you're one of the reasons I decided to write this book. Your story is proof that the doorway to our dharma never closes. It is available to us for life. By doing whatever it takes to keep living your dharma, you've given me the motivation to keep living mine.

CHAPTER THREE

PRANA

ENERGY OVER TIME

In the late nineteenth century, two strangers—one a titan in Eastern philosophy, the other a giant in Western science—happened to be in the same audience for a play headlined by French actress Sarah Bernhardt.

Both men caught Ms. Bernhardt's eye. After taking a final bow to a standing ovation, she pointed them out to her stage manager and requested that they visit her backstage. Both men showed up at the exact same time.

They couldn't have been more different. One was visiting from India—dressed in white linen and wearing a saffron-colored turban. The other was a Serbian immigrant, immaculately dressed in a three-piece suit and sporting a finely groomed mustache.

As they awkwardly waited for the actress, the Indian man broke the silence. "Hello," he said with a deep and rich Calcutta tone. "I'm Swami Vivekananda." The Serbian man extended his hand.

"Nice to meet you. I'm Nikola Tesla."

By the time the actress joined Tesla and Vivekananda, the two were locked in conversation. Vivekananda was drawing dharma frameworks in the air, while Tesla animatedly connected those principles to the scientific method. How was it possible, Tesla wondered, that these ideas were written about thousands of years ago? That's when Vivekananda introduced Tesla to a concept that would influence how Tesla saw the world.

Prana (pronounced praa-nuh).

Prana is the animating force behind your dharma. It is an energetic current that buzzes inside of you, making you feel alive and engaged. When you tap into your prana, you feel lit up, energized, and creative. When you don't, you can feel depleted, apathetic, and burnt out. The tiniest tasks can sound overwhelming, and the smallest setbacks can seem incapacitating.

Prana offers you an extraordinary source of energy, and it isn't even something you need to go find. Just like your dharma, it is already inside of you. Yet, we often ignore this natural supply of energy, relying instead on hustle and grit to squeeze more time into our schedule.

While your time is a limited resource, your prana is limitless. There are only so many hours in the day, but there's no ceiling to the creative energy you can bring to a single hour.

You and I both know what it's like to spend a lot of time on something and get very little done. We also know that one "lit up" hour can sometimes equate to a week's worth of creativity.

Robert Henri once wrote that the job of an artist isn't to make art. It is to put yourself in "that wonderful state which makes art inevitable." Prana is that wonderful state, and the purpose of this chapter is to help you tap into it.

That spontaneous meeting with Vivekananda helped Tesla

plug into his own prana. He later told audiences that if you wanted to make the most of your time, you had to think in terms of energy, frequency, and vibration. When you tap into this energy, this prana, Tesla said, "you hitch your wagon to the powers of the universe."

ENERGY OVER TIME

Hustle is an indelible part of American identity and a staple of the modern job description. We love to see it in our athletes, in our politicians, and even in our fictional characters. It is wildly inspiring to see an underdog like Rocky Balboa get bruised and bloodied (and a bit brain-damaged), yet still come out on top.

The problem is that the qualities we associate with hustle—always being on, working nonstop, being relentless—are some of the same qualities that are scientifically associated with burnout.

Sometimes it seems the path to success and the path to exhaustion look almost exactly the same. That we must choose between ambition and well-being.

The good news is that it is possible to have both, but it requires breaking out of a strict time mindset and expanding into an energy mindset.

I got my first glimpse of the power of prana when I was twelve years old. A renowned swami from South India had traveled to Michigan to speak at our temple. He was staying with a close family friend, who invited us to visit the swami before his speech that night.

On the drive there, Dad told me Swami Chinmayananda's

story. He had been a freedom fighter for India's independence and a teacher for His Holiness the Dalai Lama.

By the time we pulled into the driveway, I felt like I was about to meet a mythical hero. Our friends escorted us to the living room, where the swami was seated cross-legged on the couch. He wore the same saffron-colored robe I had recognized from religious figures in India. His long silver hair was pulled back into a bun. He wore thick glasses, and as we entered the room, he gazed softly in our direction.

My parents quickly brought their hands to prayer and bowed before him, and I followed their lead. He didn't respond with any gesture of his own but softly grunted in acknowledgment.

We took a seat in front of him and for the next few minutes sat almost entirely in silence. Then he closed his eyes. The rest of us glanced at one another, wondering whether he was asleep. Finally, my dad asked the swami about his travels. He opened his eyes halfway and said, "Theek" (fine). Then closed them again.

It was Mom's turn to engage. She asked him about the speech he would be giving that night. He unenthusiastically said, "Yes, I will be giving a speech tonight," and then he closed his eyes yet again.

What was going on here? This man had inspired millions of people. He was here in the United States for a speaking tour. In fact, he had a speech beginning in about an hour. Yet he looked like he was about to pass out.

After another uncomfortable beat of silence, I blurted out, "Are you tired, Swami?" Mom shot a horrified look in my direction, and I pretended not to notice.

The swami glacially turned his gaze toward me. Then he

cocked his head to the side and his shoulders began to gyrate up and down. I realized he was laughing. Then, with barely more than a whisper, he said something that seemed ordinary at the moment but extraordinary to me today.

"I'm conserving my energy."

By the time we reached the temple that evening, the parking lot was so jammed that we were forced to find a spot in the nearby neighborhood. When we pulled open the carved-wood temple doors, the event had already begun. My parents and I hustled to pull our shoes off and place them in cubbyholes.

That's when I heard the voice. It was thunderous, piercing, and brimming with conviction. I felt a gravitational pull to whoever was speaking. I ripped off my other shoe and walked toward the prayer hall. When I stepped into the standing-room-only space, I couldn't believe what I was seeing.

That voice was the swami's! He was seated cross-legged on the stage, his back was straight, chest open, and he leaned forward like he was about to pounce on the crowd. His hands were gesticulating with purpose. His booming voice transfixed the audience.

I realized then that the swami wasn't kidding when he said he was saving his energy. Rather than letting the energy seep out throughout the day, he pooled his prana, and then unleashed it at the precise moment when his dharma needed it the most.

RITUAL: ENERGY-MATCHING

There's a limit to how much time you can bring to a task—but there's never a limit to how much energy you can bring to a block of time. Charles Dickens wrote A Christmas Carol in about a month. *A Clockwork Orange, The Gambler,* and *On the Road* were all written within a few weeks. These authors produced great works at an incredible pace because they were so good at channeling their prana.

And you can do the same.

When examining a task, don't just consider how much time it will take—but the quality of energy it will need. Then bring awareness to the periods of your day when you feel most sharp—and *match* those to the blocks of time that need your prana the most.

Cognitive studies indicate that most of us feel more alert in the morning than in the afternoon. In those early hours, we tend to be more dialed in, better able to solve problems, and more likely to connect disparate thoughts. Early mornings tend to be primed for dharma—and yet the first thing most of us do is check our email, a task that usually doesn't require much creative energy.

For most of my life, I've been a below-average test taker. I was hoping to change that before applying to law school, so I spoke to a renowned test prep coach. He had aced both the LSAT and the MCAT but decided against going to law school or medical school. He believed that helping others get into the right schools was his dharma.

I asked him if he could share his most important piece of advice in preparing for the test. I thought he'd recommend a specific book or technique for memorizing information.

Instead, he told me to schedule the test for a time of day when I know I'm at my best. "That could make the single biggest difference in your score," he said. "The time of day you take a test can matter more than the number of hours you spend studying for it."

I later discovered an expansive study conducted in Copenhagen in collaboration with Harvard Business School. The team analyzed over two million standardized test scores to better understand how cognitive fatigue affects exam performance. For every hour after eight a.m. that a test was taken, the average score decreased by nearly 1 percent—the equivalent of missing ten days of school.

When I logged in to schedule my exam, I was surprised to see that the afternoon slots were taken, while the morning ones were wide open. I later learned that people often schedule their tests for later in the day to give themselves more time to prepare.

I would have done the same had it not been for this coach's advice. I grabbed an early slot and felt more dialed in while taking the exam. When the results arrived a couple of weeks later, I couldn't believe what I was seeing. I had, by a significant margin, received my highest-ever score on a standardized test. I hadn't developed any new skills or invested any more time in preparing for this test. I simply chose a time of day when my prana was more available.

If you feel most alert in the early morning, then thirty minutes of work in those wee hours is likely to produce more than an hour at night. If you know a weekly meeting always leaves you feeling drained, then budget time for your dharma *before* it begins instead of after it ends. On the flip side, if you know an activity—like yoga or time with a friend—is likely to inspire you, then budget some time immediately after to harness the glow.

RHYTHMIC RENEWAL

For decades we've been hearing the term *work-life balance*. Practically speaking, balance asks us to squeeze well-being into an already-packed workweek. The message is if you want to get eight hours of sleep a night or workout before the day starts, then go for it—as long as it's happening outside of business hours.

The thing about work-life balance is that it will almost always tilt in work's favor. "Workdays" are a traditional part of our daily lives; "well-being days" are not.

For too long, we've separated work from well-being despite the fact that both are essential for sustained success. People who fizzle out in their careers very rarely run out of time or talent— what they run out of is energy.

I've seen entrepreneurs shut down companies, organizations pull the plug on projects, and policymakers walk away from initiatives not because they were out of options, but because they were out of steam. They were simply too exhausted to keep going.

As it turns out, a great work ethic requires a disciplined rest ethic.

To keep their energy high, top performers don't rely on vacations or long weekends in order to reset themselves. They practice what I call rhythmic renewal. Rather than waiting for weekends or vacations, you're periodically renewing yourself with short breaks every day, throughout the day.

A day filled with breaks may sound more like the schedule of a slacker than a peak performer. But studies show us that people who achieve the highest levels of performance take somewhere around eight focused, deliberate breaks every single day.

Looking at your busy calendar, eight breaks a day might sound unrealistic, if not impossible. We've grown accustomed to a schedule that doesn't stop. By the time you end one commitment, you're already late for another.

Doing this week after week, month after month is enough to break a Buddhist monk.

Suddenly, you find yourself crashing hard. And no amount of caffeine will save you. You need a vacation, but deep down you know that won't be a long-term fix either, only a temporary escape from the energy drain. Most people report feeling more stressed one week *after* their vacation than they were before they left.

In 2018, a research paper referred to this as the "recovery paradox." It demonstrated how when our minds and bodies need to recover the most, we're less likely and less able to do anything about it. And yet, we often save our recovery periods for the moments when we feel most burnt out.

To boost your prana, you must turn recovery into a daily rhythm, rather than something you do when you feel overwhelmed. Taking small breaks might sound simple when compared to a massive problem like burnout. But it's amazing what can happen when you turn tiny breaks into a discipline.

A few years ago, I was asked to host a new docuseries on entrepreneurship, showcasing the stories of small businesses all around the world. I was a novice on camera with zero training and I felt like an impostor. By the end of the first day, the director was starting to suspect the same. We had done take after take, and each time the director coached me to "loosen up" while the other twenty members of the crew kindly tried to hide their annoyance at my incompetence.

I woke early the next morning and resolved to show up on set with the right attitude. I stretched, went to the gym, and ate a breakfast high in protein. At seven thirty a.m., I was going to be picked up by a driver. I showed up a few minutes early just to appreciate the morning sky. I was feeling as Zen as possible when my ride pulled up.

I hadn't met the driver before, but as soon as I got into his car, I could tell that he was in a bad mood. He'd been fighting rush-hour LA traffic on the way to my hotel and was about to do the same thing all over again.

He was an enormous man. His chest and biceps threatened to bust through his suit. A wraparound tattoo edged just slightly above the neckline of his white-collared shirt.

On the ride to the set, he squeezed the steering wheel tightly. He was cutting off other drivers and being cut off in return. With every lane change and sudden brake, I could feel his stress level going up.

By the time we got to our destination, his disposition had completely rubbed off on me. I was no longer loose; far from it. I unbuckled my seat belt but stopped myself from exiting. When I got out of that car, I would have to be "on," and at that moment I felt terribly off.

So I just sat there. I looked at the rearview mirror to find the driver staring at me coldly, wondering why I wasn't getting the hell out of his vehicle.

I cleared my throat. "Would it be okay with you if I just sit here for a few minutes and meditate?" His lips pursed together. He probably had to get back on the road. That's when I decided to go out on a limb. "Is there any chance you would like to join me?"

His stare intensified for a moment, but then his shoulders dropped a little. He leaned back slightly, and said with a husky, drawn voice, "Okay . . . I'll meditate with you."

I pulled out my phone and started a five-minute timer. The two of us sat together in the parking lot of the film set and just breathed. When the five minutes were up, I felt ready to walk in. I opened the car door and got out.

The driver did the same and by the time I was out of the vehicle, he was already standing in front of me. Twice my size, he pulled me into a bear hug. Then he said, "Thank you. I needed that. I *really* needed that."

He reached into his pocket and pulled out a tiny square emblem attached to a red string. Lustrous southwestern stones were pressed into its center. It looked like a small piece of a pretty mountainside.

With tenderness, he handed it to me. "I carry this on the road to keep me grounded," he said. "I want you to have it. I promise it will do the same for you today."

I looked down at the beautiful amulet now in my right palm. I told him I couldn't take it, but he insisted.

Earlier that morning, neither of us knew the other's name. On the ride over, we hadn't said anything to each other. Now he had just given me something that mattered deeply to him. We were two strangers in the middle of a busy studio lot, neither of us wanting to say goodbye.

I watched him drive away, tracing my thumb over the smooth face of the emblem. I walked onto the film set with an almost otherworldly sense of confidence.

After the first couple of takes, the director poked his head out from behind the camera equipment. "You must have slept well last night," he said.

It continued like this for the remainder of the shoot.

That driver and I never exchanged names or numbers. We haven't seen or spoken to each other since. But I carry that emblem with me everywhere. It keeps me grounded, as he promised it would. It also serves as a constant reminder of the magnificent power of a short break.

If the driver and I could reset ourselves with one focused five-minute break, what would happen if you took *multiple* breaks throughout the day?

Over the years, I have asked leaders, executives, athletes, and artists to experiment with rhythmic renewal. One of the most common pieces of feedback they give me is: "For the first time in my career, I feel more energy at the end of the day than I did at the beginning."

When was the last time you felt that way?

RITUAL: THE 55:5 MODEL

An author whose work I really admire is Anne Lamott. I keep something she wrote on my whiteboard as an important and much-needed reminder to practice rhythmic renewal. It says:

"Almost everything will work again if you unplug it for a few minutes . . . including you."

One simple way to bring rhythmic renewal into your life is through what I call the 55:5 model. It's pretty simple, really. For every fifty-five minutes of work, you take five minutes of focused, deliberate rest. You build recoveries into your day like drumbeats to a song. Instead of blocking sixty minutes to work on a project, you spend fifty-five and then do some push-ups or take a walk.

Instead of scheduling a sixty-minute meeting, you do yourself and everyone around you a favor by scheduling fifty-five minutes instead, opening up a few minutes of rest for everyone's day.

You might wonder whether these intermissions will shrink your output by reducing the amount of time you spend on work. But what the science tells us is that every single one of those five minutes will make the other fifty-five far sharper, more productive, and more creative.

So what are some five-minute recoveries that boost your energy? You can put anything you want on your "Prana List" so long as it feels like a true break, and you're doing just that one thing. You're not multitasking; you're "monotasking."

If you're having a cup of coffee, savor each sip. If you're listening to music, absorb each note. If you're taking a walk, put your phone on silent so that you can take in your surroundings.

That means you're not interrupting your break or allowing it to be interrupted by others. Set some boundaries and protect that time.

When my fifty-five minutes of work is up, I choose something from my prana list and jump right in. My favorite recoveries range from plank holds to breathing exercises to a coloring book for grown-ups. I encourage you to keep a list ready so you can take the guesswork out and build a rhythm in.

THE WORRY BREAK

One of my favorite five-minute renewals is a "worry break."

A couple of years ago I came across a senior leader who had a somewhat unusual reputation. The culture inside his company was intense and cutthroat, yet he was known for being calm and centered—while also being highly effective and well-respected.

I noticed that he carried a sand timer with him. When I asked him about it, he told me that whenever he has a worry that just won't go away, he takes his sand timer to a quiet place and turns it over.

For the next few minutes, as each grain of sand empties from one vessel to the other, he focuses on nothing but that one thing disturbing him. When his mind tries to shift to something more positive, he brings it back to worry until the timer is complete.

At first, this sounded like a recipe for anxiety. Wouldn't focusing on a troubling thought simply make it more pronounced? Neuroscience, however, tells us that *what we resist persists*. When we try to ignore or push worry out, it grows from a whisper into a scream.

According to the Cleveland Clinic, you have up to seventy thousand thoughts every single day, and researchers estimate that around 90 percent of those are duplicates of a thought you had yesterday. The majority of those duplicate thoughts also tend to skew negative. They contain at least a hint of fear, anxiety, or doubt.

If our state of mind was a soundtrack, most of us would have a song about worry playing on repeat. This doesn't just make us anxious, it drains us of energy. It's hard to be present, focused, or creative when Alice in Chains is always playing in the background.

Counterintuitively, if you focus on a single worry for a few minutes, it will likely quiet down.

My friend Cindy works for a marketing agency. She recently told me she'd been struggling to concentrate because she was constantly worried about climate change. During meetings with clients or colleagues, there's a persistent voice inside of her saying, *What does any of this matter when the planet is burning?*

So I asked her, "What if, for a few minutes each day, you allowed yourself to do nothing other than fret about climate change?" Though she was skeptical, I convinced her to give it a try for one week. About an hour before bedtime, she set a timer on her watch for five minutes and did nothing but worry about the peril facing our planet. She did this several nights in a row and started to notice something that I've observed in myself and in others.

By the time the last bit of sand drops, her catastrophic thoughts begin to quiet down. They haven't disappeared, but they're no longer demanding so much of her mental bandwidth and energy. And that has freed her up for other priorities, including getting a good night's sleep.

RITUAL: THE GRATITUDE BREAK

If focusing on one negative thought can actually make you feel better, what would happen if you intensely focused on one positive thought?

You've probably heard some of the scientifically proven benefits of gratitude. It strengthens relationships, increases feelings of security, reinforces kind behavior, and helps with depression.

It also helps boost your prana. When you feel genuine gratitude, your body tends to release oxytocin, serotonin, and dopamine— all ingredients that help shift you into a creative, energetic state of mind.

And yet, to receive gratitude's rewards, we need to do more than just think about gratitude. We need to *feel* it.

Gratitude journals have become popular, and yet listing out items can unintentionally turn gratitude into an intellectual exercise. Building an inventory might shift you to *thinking* about gratitude more than actually *feeling* it.

So I started using the sand timer for a different purpose—a gratitude break. Each night, I pick one win—big or small, personal or professional—and spend a few minutes relishing every detail of that event. Not just the victory itself, but the people and the steps that helped me along the way.

A couple of weeks ago, my six-year-old and I took a walk together around our neighborhood. We often take walks as a family after dinner, but this time the two of us went alone. Later that night, I flipped over my sand timer and took myself back to that walk. I felt her tiny hand in mine. I smelled the wind blowing off the trees that line our streets. I heard the neighborhood dogs barking in the distance. I saw porch lights turning on in the evening sky. Until the last drop of sand landed, I celebrated and relished that experience. I felt it in my bones.

Have you ever tried something like this? Most people I talk to haven't. Many of us fall into an unforgiving cycle that scientists call "hedonic adaptation." As soon as we experience any kind of success, we almost immediately reset and go looking for the next win.

In his memoir, *Confessions of a Winning Poker Player*, Jack King wrote that championship players rarely remember the hands they win. But they remember every tiny detail of the hands they lose.

We're wired to remember our losses and forget our wins.

The result is a library full of negative memories and a sparse catalog of positive ones.

So anytime you experience a setback, your brain retrieves similar negative circumstances and your mind tricks you into believing that this is part of a conspiracy-like pattern. Your internal response is, *Why does this always happen to me?* Your energy dries up and you feel depleted. You fixate on that losing hand despite the stack of chips in front of you.

Gratitude breaks are a tool to reverse our natural tendency to dismiss the wins and dwell on the losses. That might sound like a formula for happiness, but it's also an important tool for performance. Because every time you commemorate a win, you build more resilience to face the next loss.

◆ ◆ ◆

Bauji brought a legendary level of energy to his clients, his community, and his grandkids. I'll never forget playing cricket with my cousins in a quiet park in New Delhi when suddenly a loud horn broke through the silence. We all turned to see Bauji, racing toward us on a scooter, a cricket bat slung over his shoulder.

It was over a hundred degrees outside. Yet Bauji played ball until every kid on the field was utterly exhausted. Seeing our fatigue, Bauji raised his bat high in the air and heckled us with a smile.

"C'mon! You're young, act like it!"

It was during that visit to New Delhi that I began to realize that Bauji's energy didn't come naturally. It was cultivated through rhythmic recoveries, tiny rituals put on repeat.

Days before the cricket match, my parents and I had landed in New Delhi in the middle of the night. We took a three-wheeled automated rickshaw from the airport to Bauji's home.

As the only brown kid in my suburban Michigan elementary school, I had expected to arrive in New Delhi and finally feel a sense of belonging.

But the streets of Delhi felt like a totally different world to me. The aesthetics, the smell, the sounds. Tiny horns signaling lane changes, a bearded man walking the midnight road with a cane, a family of four singing by an outdoor bonfire.

Suddenly, our rickshaw driver slammed on his brakes. I looked up to see a cow slowly crossing the road. Minutes ago, our driver had berated a man for walking into traffic. But as the bovine slowly crossed our path, the driver tucked his chin to his chest and brought his hands together in prayer.

Later that night, I met over twenty members of my family for the first time. Cousins, uncles, and aunties. The door to one room was closed, and everyone pointed at it in reverence. "He's sleeping," they said.

Six of my cousins and I crowded into one room, divided between the bed and the floor. Before we turned the lights out, my cousin Seema tucked me into the bed. She pressed her forehead gently to mine and said in English, "I love you."

I had met her only minutes before, and to this day, it is one of the purest moments of affection I have ever felt.

The next morning, I woke up early to a quiet house. I got out of bed and moved past my sleeping cousins, through the open-roof hallway, and into the main family room.

There, through a stained-glass window, I saw Bauji for the

first time. He was on the front porch, holding a hot cup of chai. I could see the steam rising from the mug as he gently brought the vessel to his lips. Somehow, he noticed me spying through the window. Without even turning his head, he announced, "Come. Have a seat," gesturing to the other chair on the porch.

At our temple in Michigan, I had first heard the term *bodhisattva*. These are enlightened beings who have put off paradise to help the rest of us find a sense of peace. As I stepped out onto the porch, I looked up at my grandfather, who towered over me, even sitting down. He greeted me with such a confident, welcoming gaze that I immediately thought, *This man is a real-life bodhisattva.*

On the plane ride over, my mom had given me specific instructions.

"When you meet your elders, the first thing you do is touch their feet and ask for their blessings." I reached down to touch Bauji's feet, but he stopped me halfway down. "No need," he said, looking me in the eyes through a presence that was both strong and soft. "You already have my blessings, beta."

That morning we sat in silence, watching New Delhi wake up. We saw fruit salesmen announcing their prices into the open air, cows pulling carts through streets, and auto-rickshaws transporting people to their morning jobs. For a kid from a quiet suburb, the scene felt electric.

And yet something felt off to me. At first, I couldn't quite put my finger on it, but there was something about what Bauji was doing that seemed so different from anything I'd experienced.

Later, it hit me: he wasn't doing *anything*. He was just drinking his chai. There was no newspaper, no television, no conversation. Just him and his mug.

Back home in Michigan, our mornings were mayhem. News blaring from the TV, Mom helping me get dressed while putting breakfast on the table, Dad knotting his tie with a half-eaten bagel in his mouth, multitasking to get ahead of rush hour.

Two men, wearing finely pressed suits, emerged from the crowded Delhi street and opened the front gate to Bauji's home. They walked up to the porch and brought their hands to prayer in front of my grandfather. Then, without a single word spoken, they sat down on the grass in front of the porch. It was unusual and amusing, these two grown men in formal wear sitting cross-legged on a front lawn.

I turned to Bauji, wondering who these guys were, but didn't dare interrupt his stillness. The two men sat in silence as my grandfather continued to take slow sips from his mug. Meanwhile, several others had entered the gate to Bauji's home and found a place on the front lawn. Not a single word was uttered by any of them.

After finishing his chai and taking a few deep contemplative breaths, my grandfather turned to me and said, "Come." He stood, looking in the direction of the two men who'd arrived first. They immediately rose from the ground and followed us into the house, to Bauji's workspace. He sat behind a mahogany desk, which was positioned in front of a large shelf stacked with legal books, some of which he had authored himself.

The two men began explaining to Bauji why they were there. They were in a property dispute with a building owner that was bankrupting their business.

Bauji listened as they made their case. There was no note-taking or nodding, but it was clear that he was hearing every word. When they finished, he sprang to life. It was like a switch had been flipped on. His hands gesticulating, voice booming, he asked follow-up questions, challenged assumptions, and even cracked jokes that immediately broke the tension.

Then he pulled out a yellow legal notepad and began to write what looked like a short letter. He signed it, then suddenly boomed, "Ramu!" And out of nowhere, a well-dressed man rushed into the room, like a chief of staff entering the Oval Office. Bauji folded the yellow paper in half and told Ramu to take it directly to the landlord. The two men were overwhelmed with relief and gratitude. "Thank you, sir. Thank you!" they said repeatedly until Bauji raised his hand and, in the warmest way possible, gestured for them to leave.

This Don Corleone–like scene repeated throughout my weeks in Delhi. From morning to early evening, there always seemed to be a line of people waiting to see Bauji.

He was known for having a sharp legal mind and an incredible work ethic. One of his clients pulled me aside to tell me my grandfather was a "great man." I asked him why, and he responded that Bauji focused his total energy on every task in front of him.

"How he does anything is how he does everything."

Multiple times throughout the day, Bauji would call out to Ramu and tell him to pause the line. Ramu would signal to the waiting room on the front lawn to hold, while Bauji made his way to the porch and to the chair where I first saw him.

There, Bauji fell back to stillness. It was like a switch flipped off. Sometimes he would take a cup of chai with him, or if it was hot outside, a glass of ice water. In total silence, he carefully consumed his beverage. My cousins would often joke that Bauji drank water as if it were a fine whiskey, savoring each sip.

When he finished his drink, he'd place the mug on the side table, allow his eyes to close, and take a few deep belly breaths. Sometimes at the end of his last breath, he'd let out an "Ooommmmm," which inspired the lawn people to close their eyes, too, and absorb the richness of Bauji's deep tone.

Then he'd return to his desk.

This routine cycled throughout the day, every day. When he was at his desk, he was fully engaged with his clients. Every ounce of his energy was directed toward their cause. But on the porch, he turned the dial not halfway down, but all the way to zero. He was fully absorbed in his rest.

Those are the two Baujis I remember. One was the powerful attorney whose booming voice seemed to shake the house. And then there was the bodhisattva—the man doing absolutely nothing on his porch, except sipping from his cup with focus and intent.

It took me a long time to realize how interconnected those two really were. How those periodic moments on the porch were fueling everything else in his life.

This is what Nikola Tesla came to understand, backstage with Swami Vivekananda, and what I'd later come to understand from my interactions with the swami in Michigan. Fully expressing your dharma can only happen when you tap into your prana, that extraordinary energy that all of us have but most of us never utilize.

The path to your dharma doesn't appear through big, sweeping events. It emerges through tiny rituals practiced on repeat. Through a rhythmic pendulation of work and well-being, built into your daily life.

That drumbeat is what brings forth your most extraordinary source of energy. With that fuel, you take on meaningful projects and tackle challenging problems. You find yourself creating more with less time, because, as Tesla would say, your wagon is literally hitched to the powers of the universe.

CHAPTER FOUR

UPEKKHA

COMFORT IN THE DISCOMFORT

There's a Buddhist story I love called "Prickly Porcupine." It was a brutal winter and a group of porcupines huddled together for warmth. But the closer they got, the more they poked and needled one another. The body heat was helpful, but the pricks were painful.

Eventually, they disbanded to avoid the irritation. On their own, however, they found the harshness of the winter unbearable. They realized that running away wasn't the answer, so they returned to the huddle.

They would have to learn how to find comfort in the discomfort. To embrace a way of life that my ancestors referred to as *Upekkha* (pronounced ooh-peck-uh).

With upekkha, you're not distancing yourself from the stings of the world. You're embracing the unpleasantness with an inner evenness. Your goal isn't to create "outside space" but to cultivate "inside space."

Neurologist and Holocaust survivor Viktor Frankl wrote,

"What man actually needs is not a tensionless state but rather a striving and a struggling for a worthwhile goal."

When it comes to dharma, difficult roads can lead to brilliant destinations. If you run from the pain, you also separate yourself from possibilities.

My uncle showed me this when I was thirteen years old.

+ + +

Harkrishan Uncle had a different turban for each day of the week. Unlike some Sikh Americans, who downplayed their headwear with neutral colors, Harkrishan's turbans were bright and bold. He wore his faith proudly into workplaces, supermarkets, and especially golf courses.

Uncle picked up his first golf club as a kid in Punjab, India. Legend had it that at nine years old, he hit a two-hundred-yard drive. Word got around about Harkrishan's incredible talent, and by the time he was in high school, people were traveling from other villages to watch him play.

After immigrating to the United States, he was encouraged by local instructors to go professional, but with one child at home and another on the way, he opted instead for a steady career as an engineer. And yet he found a way to fuse his dharma into his work. He started a golf team at his manufacturing plant and led them into the finals of a major tournament. When they won, each of the Americans on the team posed for a photo wearing one of Harkrishan's turbans.

I loved Harkrishan Uncle. He was the life of the party. At weddings, he was the first person on the dance floor, luring every last one of us out there with him. At family gatherings,

Harkrishan enthusiastically told jokes that would get my parents and aunts and uncles laughing like little kids.

One morning, during the summer after seventh grade, Harkrishan Uncle showed up at the house with his golf clubs enthusiastically in hand.

"Your mom wants me to teach you how to play," he said.

Whenever Mom met someone who excelled at anything, whether it be geometry, painting, or origami, she would push my brother and me to learn from them.

Going to a golf course with Harkrishan Uncle was the absolute last thing I wanted to do. It was hard enough being the brown kid in my mostly white school. But showing up at a public course with a man in a turban? That was social suicide.

I turned to my mom and whispered, "Absolutely not!" Mom met my plea with a hard stare, and minutes later Harkrishan and I were in his car, headed to the local links.

I chewed my fingernails in anticipation. Meanwhile, my uncle was blaring his favorite Indian music on the cassette recorder. Bhangra beats resonated from a double-sided drum called the "dhol," while Harkrishan's shoulders shook in perfect unison with each note.

By the time we pulled into the parking lot, my anxiety was through the roof. I scanned the golf range for signs of anyone my age. To my relief, it was all adults . . . not a single student from Novi Middle School in sight. I finally eased up and looked over at my uncle who continued to dance until the song ended. He then turned to me with a spirited smile.

"Ready to play?"

We picked up a bucket of balls from inside the golf shop. The guy behind the counter gave my uncle a double take, his eyes focused on the turban. He had a smirk that I recognized and wondered whether Uncle did as well. I didn't ask.

We made our way to the range and found a slot. The coaching began immediately. I had played before but not with the legend himself.

After each swing, Harkrishan would place a new ball on the tee and give me an adjustment. He showed me where to position my feet, how to bend my knees, and how to use my wrists. I kept slicing the ball, curving it from left to right, away from the direction I intended.

After about twenty minutes, though, I was starting to get the hang of it. My swings were getting smoother, my contact was getting crisper. Harkrishan celebrated each hit. "That's it, my boy!" he'd say, shoulders gyrating. Now I had a smile on my face too.

That's when I heard the voice.

"Suneel Goooopta!"

It carried across the open range, capturing the attention of every customer and worker. They looked to see who it was, but I already knew. Jason Weber was in eighth grade, a year older than me, and widely known as the toughest, nastiest kid in the whole school.

Jason did not like me. That wasn't a guess. He would go out of his way to find me in the hallways at school, and once he did, he would bodycheck me into one of the lockers. I did my best to hide from him in between classes, but at least once a week I found myself bouncing off a sheet-steel locker onto the floor, my books spread around me like a mini garage sale. Jason's friends would erupt into laughter and high fives.

Jason never laughed. Instead, he would stand over me and

deliver a racially charged quip. His favorite was: "I don't like your kind."

This was 1992 and the start of the first major armed conflict with Iraq, what President George Bush Sr. named "Operation Desert Storm." It was the first time my generation saw war and it put many of my classmates into a state of fervor.

Kids in our school now had fathers and brothers fighting in the Middle East. Jason was one of them. Since he was too young to enlist himself, he decided to take his patriotic rage out on me.

Now at the golf range, Jason and his friends had a laserlike focus on Harkrishan Uncle and me. You could see Jason's mind spinning to find his sweet spot of humor and racism. Finally, he cupped his hands and shouted, "I didn't know your father was Saddam Hussein!"

I furtively glanced at my uncle, then looked away. Jason's voice was getting louder.

"Did your dad give you a ride here on his camel?"

Meanwhile, Harkrishan Uncle simply pushed a new tee halfway into the turf and set a fresh golf ball on top. Then, with zero change in tone or disposition, said, "At the end of your swing, your belt buckle should be facing the direction you want your ball to go."

I stared at my uncle in disbelief. Did he not hear what Jason had just said about him? Saddam Hussein, the camel, any of it?

I swallowed through the lump in my throat. I stepped up to the tee, brought my driver back, and took a full swing. The bottom of the club hit the top of the ball, bouncing it hard into the ground and landing it about two feet from my stance. With that, Jason and his friends lost it. One of them howled, "Golf isn't for camel jockeys!"

That was fucking it. I decided at that moment that I *had* to hit the perfect drive. Not just for me, but for every brown kid in the country. I gritted my teeth, squeezed my club, and swung at the ball with thunderous force.

Shank. The button of the club bounced against the top of the ball, driving the ball into the ground. It bounced up and rolled about a foot away from me. This sent Jason and his gang into hysterics. Meanwhile, Harkrishan Uncle simply laid down the next ball.

I tried again, and again, each time putting more force, more grit into my swing. I finally swung so hard and wild that I missed the ball altogether, losing my balance and nearly toppling to the ground.

Of course, this was comedy gold for Jason and his friends. The howls grew deeper, the slurs more piercing.

By now, the lump in my throat had swelled so much that it was hard to breathe. My eyes began to sting, begging for a tearful release. I looked at Harkrishan Uncle and with a quavering voice said, "I want to go home."

Harkrishan was kneeling to place another tee. With my words, he stopped what he was doing and gazed out at the range. I could see his heartbreak—not for himself, but for me. At that moment, he was searching for the right answer. Whether to take me home or show me a different way.

Finally, he stood up and put a gentle hand on my shoulder. "Listen, beta," he said. "This discomfort you're feeling . . . it's never really going to go away."

I looked at him with confused and angry eyes. *What did he mean? Of course* it was going to go away. Guys like Jason weren't going to follow me to college, and they certainly weren't going to follow me into the workplace. Maybe it would take another ten years, but eventually, I'd rid myself of the Jason Webers of the world.

Harkrishan, somehow reading my mind, said, "It may not be the exact discomfort you're feeling right now, but there will always be something on your path that causes you pain."

I couldn't believe what I was hearing. For all my life, Harkrishan Uncle was the guy who lived with ease, like he was dancing through life to the rhythm of a dhol drum. Now he was telling me that life was full of pain. Worse yet, that it was *never* going to go away.

I swallowed hard and repeated my request. "I just want to go home."

Harkrishan Uncle stood firm, maintaining a warm gaze. Then he said something that etched permanently into my heart.

"You can spend your life running away from discomfort. Or you can find comfort in the discomfort."

My cheeks burned. "How?" I screamed. "How can I possibly be comfortable around this kind of thing?"

"By going here." Harkrishan Uncle gently placed two fingers over my heart. "They can't touch you when you're here."

Then my uncle asked me to place both hands over my heart. Jason was watching, but at that point, things couldn't get any worse. Following Harkrishan's instructions, I closed my eyes and evened out my breath. His voice gently prompted, "In . . . out . . . in . . . out . . ."

Eyes still closed, I began to hear sprinklers in the distance. I could smell the fresh-cut summer grass and feel sunlight on my skin. The lump in my throat loosened, and my fists unclenched. I could still hear Jason, but his voice was now just a small part of a larger setting.

I opened my eyes to meet my uncle. He handed me my club. I wrapped my fingers around it, this time with a looser grip. I stepped up to the tee, positioned my stance, and locked my attention on the ball. I pulled the driver back up and over my shoulder.

What happened next still plays back in slow motion. I took a deep breath, and as I uncoiled, every bit of hurt, heartbreak, love, and hope exhaled through me.

My swing created a mystical-sounding *whoosh* and connected with the golf ball in a high-pitched click that sent a shiver down my spine. The tiny sphere soared deep into the range. It climbed higher and higher, eventually descending and bouncing into the turf, advancing in the exact direction my belt buckle pointed.

As the ball gracefully rolled down its path, the laughter faded away.

Harkrishan beamed, put his hands in the air, and did a little shoulder shake. Then he reached into the bucket to grab another ball.

THE SPACE BETWEEN

Harkrishan Uncle wisely predicted that Jason Weber never really goes away. He simply changes form.

Passive-aggressive coworkers, overbearing supervisors, impossible-to-please clients. Bad drivers. Kids complaining.

Needy friends. These are what psychologists call triggers, and you can't hide from them.

That doesn't mean we don't try. But just like the porcupines, we escape one challenge and find another one around the corner. Maybe you quit a job you enjoy because your boss is a pain, only to find that the commute of your next job is jammed with unexpected traffic.

Harkrishan laid out the choices: we can run away from the pain, or we can learn to find comfort in the discomfort.

In *Man's Search for Meaning*, Viktor Frankl chronicled his experiences as a prisoner inside a Nazi concentration camp. Even in the depths of his own suffering, Frankl couldn't help but observe the mindsets of his fellow prisoners. For those who didn't break, what was it that gave them strength?

Frankl discovered their primary motivation wasn't to escape the pain. It wasn't to avoid the strife and struggle. Their success came from finding an *inner space* between difficulty and response.

After a lifetime of reflecting on the harshest human conditions possible, Frankl concluded that in between an impulse and your response is a gap, and within that space lies your freedom.

The key to creating inner space isn't to block emotion. It isn't even necessary to control your emotions but rather to ensure that your emotions aren't controlling you.

Author Robin Rice calls this "wedge work"—you're literally putting a wedge in between stimulus and response. She calls this "the half inch between heaven and hell." This does *not* mean you're "OMMing your way through real problems," says Rice. "Anger is real. It's natural. And I believe it's holy, in the right expression."

With a wedge in place, you're not removing your anger. You're getting skilled at managing it. Pretend for a moment that when something makes you angry, a fuse is lit, and when the fuse reaches its end, you explode. We can spend a lifetime trying to get rid of our inner explosives. But even the most disciplined practitioners experience anger.

Thich Nhat Hanh was a beloved Vietnamese monk and teacher, a symbol of peace and calm, and even he admitted to having frequent feelings of irritation and even anger. But Thich Nhat Hanh had built in enough upekkha, enough inner space, to not act from that place.

Our mission isn't to remove your explosives, but rather to lengthen your fuse. To create more distance between the start and end of the wick. That extra time gives you space. That space gives you choices. And those choices give you freedom.

RITUAL: FIND YOUR HOME BASE

It's easy to create space when you're in the middle of a bubble bath. What about when you're in the heat of the moment, feeling pressured by a boss or being sniped at by a family member?

At the golf range, Harkrishan Uncle's ritual was to have me put both hands over my heart and take a few breaths. To this day, that remains one of my go-to upekkha tools.

However, I often find myself in situations where closing my eyes and placing my hands over my heart would be awkward. Can you imagine doing that in the middle of a meeting? I tried once. People stopped what they were doing and asked if I was okay.

What I've since realized is that you don't need a physical

gesture to find inner peace. Without anyone noticing, you can quickly take your attention to a home base.

Nazi guards told Viktor Frankl where to stand, where to dig, and where to kneel. He never had the option of calling a "time-out." So he'd imagine himself speaking at a podium in a "well-lit, warm and pleasant lecture room." Frankl described the scene:

"In front of me sat an attentive audience on comfortable up-holstered seats. I was giving a lecture on the psychology of the concentration camp! All that oppressed me at that moment be-came objective, seen and described from the remote viewpoint of science. By this method, I succeeded somehow in rising above the situation, above the sufferings of the moment, and I observed them as if they were already of the past."

Your home base is always available to you. This could be as simple as paying attention to your breath for a few seconds. Or it could be a memory, like that of a stream you enjoyed playing at when you were a kid. For just a brief moment, you can recall the ripples, the sounds, the laughter. In a high-pressure situation, you can travel there even for a quick moment to reset yourself.

This is what Harkrishan Uncle meant when he pointed to my heart and said, "They can't touch you when you're here."

GETTING CURIOUS INSTEAD OF FURIOUS

When you're genuinely curious, you can't really be furious. It's impossible for those two states to coexist. You have to choose one or the other.

I have a friend whom I really enjoy spending time with, but

he has a habit of one-upmanship. Every time I share something, Andrew comes in with something to top it. To make matters worse, he's obnoxiously successful, so he has no shortage of content to work with.

Now when Andrew is one-upping me, I visualize a fork in the road. In one direction is "furious" and in the other direction is "curious." I imagine myself turning down the road of curiosity and allowing questions to silently come to mind.

Typically, two questions come up.

The first is: What made *him* this way? Perhaps it has something to do with how he grew up. Maybe Andrew was constantly assaulted by successful siblings, eager to outshine one another. Or maybe he had extremely difficult-to-please parents. I don't know for sure, but in this state of curiosity, I allow for those kinds of possibilities.

The second question is: What made *me* this way? In other words, what is it about one-upmanship that triggers me so much? When I chase that question down, the answer I usually find is that I have a deep-seated desire to prove myself in the eyes of others—to friends, to colleagues, and to Jason Weber.

You might be thinking, if I follow my curiosity right in the middle of a conversation, won't that make me distant or aloof? Maybe a little, but being curious is far less distracting than getting furious. And it only takes a brief moment to ponder a question and then return to the moment.

One thing I've realized is that the road to curiosity almost always leads to compassion for the other person. I can genuinely see the possibility of Andrew sitting at his dinner table, feeling dismissed and belittled. I'm not sure if that happened, but I truly wonder if it did, and that wonder alone gives me some comfort.

RITUAL: A SHORT FUSE FOR KINDNESS

There are times when having a short fuse is helpful. If my five-year-old is running toward high-speed traffic, that isn't a moment for me to get curious. I need to act quickly and protect her safety.

A short fuse can also be useful when you have something kind to share. Sometimes it's best to act quickly on generosity before the moment passes and you get pulled into something else.

I asked Ben Cohen (the Ben in Ben & Jerry's) what he's learned most about being a leader. He said to "catch people doing something right." As leaders, we're trained to catch people doing something wrong. He does the opposite.

I've found that attitude useful in all areas of life.

In the past, I had a short fuse for anger but a long fuse for kindness. I was quick to react to something that bothered me but slow to pay someone a compliment. Or if a friend popped to mind and I felt compelled to call them, I often wouldn't, instead making a mental note to phone them later.

My goal now is to reverse the fuses. To act fast on positive emotions and slowly on negative ones. To be slow with anger and quick with kindness.

Next time you get the impulse to catch up with an old classmate, colleague, or even your mom—go with it. Make the call. They'll be glad you did and so will you.

LOOSENING YOUR GRIP

As you know by now, I was kind of a mess after selling my healthcare company. I had spent the past several years working nonstop and, even after a successful sale, I could not find a way to relax and reset. I was completely burnt out, impulsive, and irritable.

A concerned friend recommended a seven-day silent meditation retreat at a Buddhist monastery. Lance promised that after three days of silence, I would feel a return to calm. After five days, I would see more beauty and joy around me. By the seventh day, I would be fully ready to return to the outside world with a rested disposition.

That sounded almost too good to be true. And unfortunately, it was. Nothing Lance had promised was happening for me. I found the silence deafening, and the endless meditation was more than I could mentally and physically handle.

On day three, I cracked. After one of our meditation sittings, I sprint-walked to my tent and pulled pen and paper out of my backpack. I quickly drafted a note: "I'm sorry I can't complete the retreat. Can I get a ride to the bus stop this evening?"

I found one of the monks and gave him the note. He took the message with a serene look on his face and read it impassively. The monk then tucked the piece of paper into his robe and walked away. I stood there, confused and annoyed by the interaction. Should I have brought a pen for him to write a response?

When I opened my eyes after our next meditation, I found a new piece of paper in front of me. I unfolded the note, which informed me that someone would give me a lift to the bus stop that evening. "Before you leave," it continued, "the abbot would like to see you. Please go now to his home on the hill."

I began a slow walk up a steep incline toward the head monk's home and arrived, slightly winded, at a picket fence surrounding a beautifully manicured lawn. I unlatched the gate and advanced on stone steps to the front porch.

I tried to peek through a screen door, when a deep voice boomed from inside, startling me: "Come on in!"

I walked into a home that reminded me of my grandmother, who had emigrated from India to suburban Michigan. The decor was a Midwestern mix of East and West. Magnificent Buddha statues rested on linoleum flooring. An IKEA couch pressed up against a wall with ancient artifacts.

Dressed in a slightly more deluxe robe than the other monks, the abbot was standing over the stove in an open-faced kitchen. He was wearing thick-framed glasses and had an amused look on his face, a spirit that instantly reminded me of the Dalai Lama.

"I'm making us tea!" he boomed again.

For the past two days, not a word had been allowed. But the abbot was speaking to me like we were sitting in the stands of a baseball game. He filled two round mugs with clear steaming tea and then gently lifted each onto a small tray.

"Let's sit," he said. I was sore from time spent in the meditative position and relieved when he waved me over to the couch. He placed one of the mugs on a coffee table in front of me. I sat down and he found his way to a La-Z-Boy recliner across the tiny table. He pulled the recliner back, exposing the bottoms of his Teva sandals.

Thrown off by the entire setting, I scanned the living room and the photos on the wall. There were pictures of him meditating in monasteries, hiking in the Himalayas, and lecturing in front of robed men. One photo stood out from the rest: It was the abbot next to a Formula 1 race car. He was in a stadium, with fans in the stands and a helmet in his hand. It was clear from the image that *he* had just raced the car.

The abbot watched me wonder from across the room, slowly

sipping his tea. I reached for my mug as well. It didn't have a handle, so I gripped my hands around each side. Suddenly I felt a sting in my palms. I winced, dropping the hot mug back onto the table. It landed in a loud clang, upright, but with the overflow spilling onto the table.

"Sorry," I said, inspecting my burning palms.

The abbot chuckled warmly, gesturing that it was okay. That's when I realized that he was holding the exact same type of mug with total ease. I watched him bring the tea to his lips, sip it carefully, and return the mug to his lap. I was puzzled, and he clearly noticed.

"Pick up your mug again," he said. "But this time, pick it up lightly. Create a little space between your hands and the cup." Sensing my hesitation, he assured me further, "Hold it lightly, not tightly."

I carefully picked up the mug, holding the sides as loosely as the laws of friction would allow. I felt the heat this time, but it wasn't piercing. I slowly raised the mug and blew a layer of steam off the top. Then I gently pressed my lips to the outer edge, taking in my first sip of jasmine.

I looked up at the abbot. He was now leaning forward in his chair. Gazing at me warmly, he said, "Whenever life feels intense, our natural instinct is to tighten our grip. We want to fight the intensity with intensity." He continued, "But if you squeeze a hot mug, you burn your hands. So . . . the more intense things become, the *less* intensely we must react."

I set down the mug once more, leaned back on the sofa, and folded my arms. I was a little annoyed by the lesson. For years in the startup world, I had been told by friends and family to "stop and smell the roses." But had I taken my foot off the gas, even for a minute, would we have succeeded?

So in a moment that I'm not particularly proud of, I got snippy with a Buddhist monk. "What you're saying is not to work hard, not to try hard. But I want to succeed. I like having ambition and drive. What you're telling me is that those things don't matter."

He slowly arched his eyebrows in response to my tiny tantrum. "Not at all," he said gently.

He then pointed to the photo of the racetrack. "One of the first things you're taught in racing is to loosen your grip. On a scale of one to ten, you never hold your wheel at more than a five."

The abbot went on to explain that if your grip is tight, you miss feedback from the car and road, and that leads to errors in judgment. Counterintuitively, the faster the speed and the tighter the turns, the looser your grip needs to be in order to succeed.

Picking up his hot mug, the abbot continued, "Loosening your grip doesn't make you less ambitious. It means you care deeply about what's in your hands."

With that, the abbot's next guest arrived at the screen door and he boomed from his recliner, "Come on in!" I stood up and apologized for snapping at him. "You were snapping at me?" he asked, genuine surprise in his voice.

I thanked him for the tea, and he smiled warmly. "Loosen your grip and you'll go farther than you imagined."

♦ ♦ ♦

From a young age, it was clear that playing baseball was Hank Aaron's dharma. Growing up poor in 1940s Alabama, his family couldn't afford proper equipment, so he'd fashion his own bats and balls out of everyday items. With no baseball fields nearby, he'd round up the neighborhood kids to play in the street.

Pulling him away from a game in progress was no small task. However, when Aaron's mother shouted from the window, "Get under the bed!," Aaron dropped his makeshift bat and raced home as fast as he could. His mother locked the door behind him, and they hid in the darkened house.

A few minutes later, Aaron would crawl out from underneath his bed to peek out the window, where he'd see a group of men marching past their home. They were dressed in white hoods, and the man in front held up a burning cross. The moment the Klan was out of sight, Aaron was back on the street, rallying his friends to resume their game.

As a boy, Aaron was already learning to find comfort in the discomfort. Over the coming years, his sense of upekkha would come under heavier fire.

Aaron made his big league debut in 1954, at twenty years of age. Nineteen years later, he was considered one of the best to play the game. Babe Ruth was still considered the greatest of all time, thanks to his 714 career home runs, widely viewed as the most hallowed and unbreakable record in all of sports.

As Aaron entered the 1973 season, he was only forty-one home runs shy of breaking Ruth's record. Not a huge deficit, but he was already thirty-nine years old, an age where the body can easily break down over the grind of a 162-game season. But Aaron's body cooperated and he kept knocking the ball out of the park. By midseason, it was clear that the Babe's record was in real danger.

You might think that Aaron's home run chase was something the entire country would rally behind. Instead, it stoked racial tensions in an already-divided nation. White America considered Babe Ruth to be one of their own and the face of baseball. Most of them did *not* want to see a Black man shattering their hero's record.

By late summer, Aaron was receiving a countless amount of hate mail every day. Many of these contained death threats— *if you beat Babe Ruth's record, you will die.* Some envelopes even contained detailed schematics of gunfire pointed at Hank as he stood in the batter's box. Others showed how he would be shot rounding the bases before reaching home plate.

It's worth remembering that in 1973, assassinations of public figures were still fresh in the country's mind. It had only been a few years since Bobby Kennedy and Dr. Martin Luther King were murdered. The Ku Klux Klan was also still very active and rallying racists everywhere to protect Ruth's record from a Black man. The threats were so serious that the FBI got involved and Aaron's team assigned bodyguards to protect him.

And yet no one could really protect Aaron on the field. Each time he stepped up to the plate was like setting foot in enemy territory. Hateful slurs filled the air. Clanging and banging noises echoed across the stadium, heightening the anticipation of an attack.

Aaron's teammates recount how in these moments, their eyes would scan the stadium seats for gunmen, their own hands trembling with fear. And yet, when it was Aaron's turn at bat, he would simply walk to the plate, line up his feet, hips, and shoulders, and wrap his fingers loosely around the bat.

What was happening at that moment was a picture of upekkha. Assaults and threats were being hurled at Aaron from every direction. And while he couldn't control what was happening around him, he knew he could control what was happening inside. Aaron understood that there was a distance between impulse and response, and inside that space was his freedom.

Aaron said that once he put on his uniform, he created that wedge between the death threats and his dharma as a ballplayer. He reminded himself that matching outside pressure with inside severity wouldn't improve his performance. With a loose grip, he went to his inner home base, and a mantra that always kept him focused.

Always keep swinging. Focus on each at bat, each pitch, and each step. Find comfort in the discomfort.

This attitude couldn't protect Aaron from the outside scars he endured. There's nothing that can ever remove that stain from American history. And yet, the spirit of upekkha was with him from his days as a child escaping the KKK to a fabled night on April 8, 1974. Hank Aaron stepped up to home plate inside Atlanta-Fulton County Stadium at 9:07 p.m. Every player on the bench, every fan in the sold-out stadium, and everyone watching from home was restless with anticipation. Aaron was now only one home run shy of breaking Babe Ruth's record.

While the stadium pulsated with fear and suspense, Aaron calmly walked to the plate and took his stance. The first pitch was low, and Aaron resisted the temptation to swing. The pitcher narrowed his eyes, wound up, and released his second throw.

I still remember the sound of my golf club making contact with the ball that day with Harkrishan Uncle. If I close my eyes, I can feel the tingle in my spine. And I can still see the stunned look on Jason Weber's face.

When Aaron's bat connected with that pitch, a sharp and resonant sound pierced the air, bringing every slur to silence.

The ball soared 385 feet, and over the left-field wall. Fans slowly rose to their feet and began to accept, applaud, and even cheer Aaron as he rounded the bases.

Broadcaster Vin Scully described the scene that night. "A Black man is getting a standing ovation in the Deep South for breaking a record of an all-time baseball idol. What a marvelous moment for baseball. . . . What a marvelous moment for the country and the world."

And, of course, what a marvelous day for Hank Aaron's dharma.

CHAPTER FIVE

LEELA

HIGH PLAY

When Phil Jackson played in the NBA, he had his favorite mantra taped to the inside of his locker: "Make your work your play and your play your work."

Those words would later become the core of Jackson's philosophy as a head coach. He believed that if he could get his players to spend less time obsessing over winning, and more time connecting with "the intrinsic joy of the game," two things would happen. Work would begin to feel like play. And counterintuitively, that would lead to even better work.

Jackson was regularly mocked by commentators and coaches for his "hippy vibes" but no one could deny his results. He led his teams to an incredible eleven championships and shaped the careers of legends like Michael Jordan and Kobe Bryant.

My ancestors would have described Jackson's approach to life and coaching as *Leela* (pronounced lee-lah), which translates to "high play." When you're in a state of leela—work feels like play, and play feels like work. You're having fun and also performing at levels that previously seemed unobtainable.

Leela runs counter to what we've been taught, right? Play is what you do when you *aren't* working. And there's a certain way to think and behave when you're working, which is entirely different from the ways to think and behave when you're playing.

What Jackson demonstrated, and science has backed, is that blurring the lines between work and play is more than a recipe for happiness—it's a recipe for success.

◆ ◆ ◆

The late scientist Mihaly Csikszentmihalyi may have described leela as being in a state of "flow." One of Csikszentmihalyi's great contributions to science was in showing how each of us has both an "exotelic" and an "autotelic" side to our personalities.

Your exotelic side wants you to achieve things, whereas your autotelic side wants you to *feel* things. Your exotelic side cares more about the outcome, your autotelic side cares more about what you experience along the way. You aren't one or the other, but shades of each. The question is which one dominates the other.

Until Csikszentmihalyi came along, most of us assumed that peak performers skewed exotelic. That what drove them to success was an unshakable desire to achieve a result.

Csikszentmihalyi showed, however, that at the highest levels of society—from business to athletics to the arts—you will also find people who lean autotelic. It's not that they don't care about goals or victories, but they're driven more by a desire to *experience* things than a desire to achieve things. And that, in turn, leads them to accomplish even more.

Mountaineer Alex Lowe once said that "the best climber in the world is the one who's having the most fun."

When you adopt a leela mindset, you're not just out there following your bliss. You still care deeply about the quality of your work; it's just that the work itself feels like the reward. When that happens, work and play feel less like a balancing act and more like a partnership.

Philosopher L. P. Jacks said that a master in the art of living is hardly able to recognize the distinction between work and play. "He simply pursues his vision of excellence at whatever he does, leaving others to decide whether he is working or playing. To him, he's always doing both."

In this chapter, we're going to learn how to make your work feel like play—and in doing so, step into an even more fulfilling expression of dharma.

THE ROLE IS THE REWARD

When it comes to work, you have a "goal," and you have a "role." Your goal is what you want to achieve. Your role is the work you do to get there. The goal is the outcome you hope to create. The role is all the experiences you'll have along the way.

Which one should be in the driver's seat, the role or the goal?

In middle school, Deena Kastor fell in love with running. Through the trails in the Santa Monica Mountains, she developed a new relationship with nature. As her heart rate rose, the greens seemed brighter, the blues felt deeper, and the texture of the trail sounded crisper.

She was only eleven years old, but Kastor knew that running would channel her competitive spirit and nourish her internally for life. It was her dharma.

Kastor became an elite runner. She shattered records, earned a full scholarship to college, and eventually became a serious contender for the Olympic team. As her star—and the stakes—kept rising, the lines between work and play became more distinct.

In the past, track meets felt like community gatherings—an opportunity to connect and compete with friends.

Now they felt like do-or-die events. Every practice was in preparation for the next meet. The weight of everyone's expectations, especially her own, was bringing her down. She began to feel alienated from the very activity that had once given her a sense of purpose and belonging. It was all work and no play. The pressure continued to mount and all she felt was burnout.

So as her junior year of college approached, and her Olympic aspirations were about to materialize, Kastor did something that shocked her team, her friends, and even her immediate family. She took the year off.

Junior year is a critical time for a university athlete who wants to go pro. By sitting out that season, she was essentially closing the door on her dream. But Kastor felt a wave of relief. There was a new pep in her step as she walked around campus, happy in the knowledge that another grueling practice was no longer waiting around the corner.

In some ways, Kastor's story resembles the tales of the people in ancient India who fled to the forests during the Great Renunciation. They were looking for an escape from the mounting pressure of civilized life, and they found it.

But like them, it didn't take long for Kastor to miss what she had left behind. While Kastor's life had become less stressful, she missed the rush of racing, the camaraderie of running with others, and the thrill of competition.

As much as she wanted to escape, she knew deep down that running was her dharma and her destiny.

Like those people in the forest so long ago, Kastor found herself in a mental and emotional trap. Running gave her crippling anxiety, but it also filled her with joie de vivre.

She wished that she could reconnect with the feeling she had as a kid in the Santa Monica Mountains. That was the only time in her life when work and play didn't feel like opposites but complements.

There's a saying in the East: When the student is ready, the teacher appears. When Kastor felt open to a new beginning, a coach named Joe Vigil entered her life.

Like Phil Jackson, Vigil was eccentric by coaching standards. Unlike his contemporaries, he had spent a lot of time overseas, including studying runners in Africa. He wanted to understand how they performed, and more importantly, how they practiced.

What Coach Vigil saw surprised him. The winningest runners seemed to be focused more on the joy of racing than they were on the act of winning. An American sports agent once summarized this nicely. Americans "race with anxiety," he said, while Kenyans "enjoy the battle."

Coach Vigil noticed this difference everywhere he looked. American training facilities were built around numbers: how far to run, which milestones to hit, and how many seconds could be shaved in order to win. Training for a race felt a lot like building a business with charts, goals, and precise metrics.

African teams, on the other hand, rarely used devices to measure output. Instead, they tuned in to their own body for guidance. In the middle of a race, if their body said it was time to slow down, they intentionally decreased their pace in order to regain strength. When their body felt rested enough, they'd break out with intensity.

For these runners, the lines between work and play felt subtle, if not invisible. It wasn't that they didn't want to win medals, but they loved the act of running even more.

For them, the role itself was the reward. The irony is that, in turn, they were winning more rewards.

From the early '80s into the 2000s, African teams were on an unprecedented winning streak, taking home dozens of Olympic medals. Meanwhile, no American distance runner had medaled in that time span.

Vigil decided he needed to reboot the way he trained athletes. He needed to blur the lines between work and play. He did this by emphasizing the difference between "excellence" and "success." Excellence represented the role, and success represented the goal. Pursue excellence, Vigil would say, and success will inevitably follow.

When Kastor met Coach Vigil in 1996, she saw someone who could help her recapture those feelings of childhood wonder. A coach who could help her align outer and inner success.

At practice, Vigil showed Kastor and her teammates how to intentionally lose track of how many miles they ran, and instead tune in to the feeling of running hard and long. The goal was to leave the track internally satisfied. To have fun, and stay connected to what made them want to run in the first place.

By blurring the lines between work and play, Kastor reconnected with her joy of running. She was taken back to the sights and sounds she loved as a kid: the trickling of gentle rivers, the sounds of hidden wildlife playing. She was waking up early again, finding new trails to run, and discovering new climbs to master.

Kastor's leela mindset led to breakthrough results.

In 2004, she won America's first Olympic medal for long-distance running in nearly forty years. And in 2006, Kastor won the London Marathon. She completed that race in less than two hours and twenty minutes, which made her the fastest female marathoner in American history.

RITUAL: HIGH-QUALITY HABITS

F. M. Alexander once said that we don't decide our future. We decide our "habits" and our habits decide our future.

We live in a society, though, that fixates on outcomes and dismisses the habits that get us there. In the workplace, leaders often tell their teams "I don't care how it gets done, just that it gets done." In school, we're evaluated purely on how we perform on a test and not how we prepare for it.

The result is a collective mindset of "doing whatever it takes" to hit a goal, even if the path to get there is joyless.

My startup, RISE, coached thousands of people who were trying to lose weight. People would often sign up for the service looking to make a wholesale change in their diet, such as eliminating carbs. Our clients loved pasta and bread, but they saw doing away with them as a fast track to success.

The problem with a joyless diet is that every day feels like a slog. And even if you get results, they typically vanish when your willpower inevitably runs dry.

On the other hand, when our customers found a habit that they actually enjoyed, they were much more likely to not only lose the weight but keep it off. For example, drinking a glass of water before each meal was one of the most effective weight loss habits we witnessed.

It may sound overly simple, but drinking water before every meal makes you feel less hungry and therefore less likely to overeat. The extra hydration keeps you energized and satiated throughout the day. It's also great for your skin.

Unlike those who completely cut out carbs, people didn't see hydration as a chore; many of them even found it to be fun. They bought water bottles with inspiring quotes and time markers. They infused fruit and experimented with new forms of electrolytes.

Kevin Kelly, the founding editor of *Wired*, says don't aim for better ways to do your tasks, "aim for better tasks that you never want to stop doing."

I refer to these types of tasks as "high-quality habits."

Deena Kastor used high-quality habits to bring back joy to her running routine. She bought pretty water glasses to make hydrating more appealing. She would place lavender from the garden in her shoes to make them more comforting to put on in the morning.

Instead of obsessing over an outcome, ask yourself what high-quality habit would lead to the result. What's something that you would enjoy doing on repeat that would also make success more inevitable? Then focus on that.

THE MUSIC MINDSET

Philosopher Alan Watts would say, "You *play* the piano, you don't *work* the piano." The point of play isn't to get through it quickly, just as the final note of a symphony isn't the point of a symphony. "If that were so," said Watts, "the best conductors would be the ones who play the fastest. And there would be composers who only wrote finales."

As kids, I think we're wired with a "music mindset." We're not trying to get to the end of the song—because we're having too much fun with the notes in between. As we get older, we tend to lose that mindset and focus purely on outcomes. The lines between work and play become much more pronounced.

It is possible, even as adults, to regain our music mindset. And when that happens, we find our work much more fulfilling. We also increase our capacity for creativity and service. And that leads to even better results.

Embracing a music mindset doesn't require you to learn new tools, but to let go of existing ones. Remember, Michelangelo saw his craft as the art of removing things, not adding things. The same is true with leela. We are literally chiseling away the boundaries of work and play.

Expectations are perhaps the most important element for you to chisel away. They are the lethal enemy of leela. Expectations define and make bold the lines between work and play. They turn the thrill of winning into the fear of not receiving an expected benefit.

Expectations are a joy killer. As soon as you have them, you get ripped right out of the music mindset. Because if the reason you're performing a task is for some expected future value, then you can't be completely absorbed in the task itself. You can't enjoy each note fully because your energy is subdivided between the goal and the role.

We sometimes believe that having expectations and having ambition are one and the same. But there's a difference. Ambition is something you want, whereas an expectation is something you feel entitled to. Ambition is an acknowledgment of desire, whereas expectations are an illusion of control. Ambition is thrilling and can be inherently playful, whereas expectations suck the fun out of an experience.

When you expect something to happen and it doesn't, you get disappointed. Get disappointed one too many times, and you become disillusioned. And when you're disillusioned, you're much more likely to disengage from whatever path you are on, even if that path is leading straight to your dharma.

RITUAL: HOW TO AVOID DISAPPOINTMENT

Jimi Hendrix would say that his primary goal as a performer was to "turn people on."

A reporter once asked Hendrix what happened when he *didn't* achieve that goal. What happened when he looked out at his audience and found that they weren't being turned on?

"If they respond, then it gives me energy. But if they don't respond, well, then I play for myself."

Now Hendrix obviously cared about the audience's reaction—

he just didn't *depend* on it. He had ambition, but he didn't have expectations.

This gave Hendrix a mental plan B. If audiences weren't responding, then he could always fall back to a fail-safe purpose—playing music for himself. No matter how the audience responded, Hendrix could use the stage to try new things and go deeper into his craft.

Having a mental backup plan is essential to removing expectations and entering a state of leela. If you create an alternate tunnel to take when things aren't going right, you free yourself of the belief that things *should* go a certain way or be a certain way. So even when things don't turn out the way you want, you can still continue to perform, create, and play.

Give it a try: In your next challenging situation, create a mental plan B. If things don't go as planned, know what you're going to tell yourself. This simple practice will loosen the stronghold of expectations. You may be surprised how far that extra hit of energy and resilience will take you.

◆ ◆ ◆

Throughout most of high school, I was what the doctors called "clinically obese." To hide my weight, I'd raid my dad's closet for baggy clothes. This disguise wasn't winning me any style points, but it did keep some of the fat jokes at bay. Then, just before the start of junior year, I received a letter from the school that threatened to blow my cover.

It was a reminder that I had not yet taken the required "swimming class." Of course, I already knew this. I had no intention of enrolling in a class that would make me strip down in front of my classmates. Now the school was telling me I had no choice.

In the weeks leading up to class, I was hyperfocused on my goal of losing weight. I attempted every diet I could think of. I stopped eating fat, then after seeing no results, I gorged on fatty foods and removed all carbs. But no diet gave me the instant progress I expected and the frustration of it all had me scarfing down buckets of mint chocolate chip ice cream.

On the first day of swim class, I sprinted to the locker room to make sure I got there before anyone else. I quickly shed my clothes and threw my swimsuit on. I then pulled out an oversize beach towel from a paper bag and wrapped it around my body like a toga. By the time my classmates arrived, I was already seated cross-legged next to the indoor pool like a rotund Roman emperor.

That's when Ms. Tomanek explained that this first day was an "assessment." Each of us would do a timed lap to the end of the pool and back. One by one. That meant there would be a single point in time when all eyes would be on my togaless body.

We moved alphabetically. When the teacher called out the name "Davis," only a couple of letters away from "Gupta," I felt like I was having a panic attack. The humidity in the room felt stifling, my toga pulled a little closer to my skin, and the smell of chlorine burned my nostrils.

"Gupta." The sound of my last name reverberated for a moment and was then swallowed into the sticky air. I stared at Ms. Tomanek, silently pleading with her to call this off. Her face expressed nothing. I dropped my towel. She looked away.

I scurried toward the pool and slipped into the water. I was relieved not to hear laughter. Ms. Tomanek blew her whistle and I began to paddle.

I made it to one end, then kicked off the side to return back to the starting point. That's when it hit me. Walking toward the pool had been the easy part. Now I was going to have to stroll back *toward* everyone, dripping wet, without the protection of my toga.

I slowly climbed the ladder out of the pool, sucking my belly button in as tight as it would go. I took one stilted step after another toward the group. No one said a word, they just stared. And stared.

Finally, a redheaded kid pointed his finger at me and shouted: "You've got bigger tits than most of the girls in this school!"

The room exploded in laughter.

My cheeks burned for the rest of class, the rest of that day, and, as far as I remember, the rest of the school year. But after that experience, I decided that somehow, someway, I was going to lose weight. I didn't have a plan, but I had a goal, one I was more committed to than ever before.

That summer I enrolled in an eight-week writing camp in Evanston, Illinois. My parents drove the four hours from Detroit to drop me off at the dorm where I'd be spending the next two months.

I got there early on the first day, hiding out in the lower-middle half of the classroom, watching all the new faces stroll in. Gene's was the one that captured my attention—and everyone else's. He was tall and built, wearing a varsity jacket with a wrestling patch.

While there were plenty of seats available, Gene chose the one right next to me. I squirmed a little, put my mechanical pencil in my mouth, and pretended to look in the other direction.

"Hi . . . my name is Gene," he said to me. I looked at him nervously, wondering whether he needed something. "Uh . . . is this seat reserved for one of your friends?" I asked. "Because I could go somewhere else."

Gene laughed. "No, that's your seat . . . you're pretty funny," he said.

From that day on, Gene and I were inseparable. At least, I never really left his side, and he didn't seem to mind. He told me what it was like to be a competitive wrestler, and I shared what it was like to have never participated in any formal athletic activity. We were fascinated by each other.

One day after class, Gene and I took the long route back to our dorm, walking by Lake Michigan. That's when I told him something I had never admitted out loud, not even to my parents. "Gene . . . I want to lose weight."

He didn't respond. We just continued walking, both of us staring ahead.

"Six a.m.," said Gene, breaking the silence.

"What?"

"Be ready tomorrow . . . at six a.m."

"Be ready for what?" I asked.

"To run," he said.

In eighth-grade gym, our whole class was forced to run a mile. I finished dead last and vowed never to run again. Now, this guy was asking me to do so voluntarily. Sure, my goal was to lose weight, but not like this. We continued to walk in silence, and I tried to formulate the right way to object to this plan. Nothing came to me.

That next morning, at six on the dot, there was a knock at my door. I opened it and on the other side was Gene in shorts, a T-shirt, and running shoes. A few minutes later, we were walking toward Lake Michigan again.

And then, Gene broke out into a brisk jog. I did the same.

The discomfort set in quickly. My lungs began to burn, and

I could taste the bile in the back of my throat. I told Gene that my stomach was starting to cramp. He just kept running. I felt like I had no choice but to keep up the pace. I ran two miles that day. The farthest I'd ever gone. When we arrived at our dorm, I vomited into the bushes.

When I was finished, Gene put a hand on my shoulder. "Tomorrow . . . six a.m."

For the next few days, I dragged myself out of bed before dawn, which felt like the hardest thing I had ever done in my life. I kept reminding myself that if this is what it took to achieve my goal, it'd be worth it. A week later, my eyes opened before the alarm clock sounded. I wasn't jumping out of bed, but I wasn't dragging, either. Each morning, I was answering the door a little quicker, until one morning Gene rounded the corner and found me stretching in the hallway.

Six a.m. runs with Gene became my high-quality habit. It didn't matter how I felt. It didn't matter if it was raining. It didn't matter if we had a quiz later that morning. It was something I *wanted* to do.

To be honest, I wasn't noticing any significant weight loss. But I didn't even think about it much. After running, I felt more confident. Proud. I was walking into morning class feeling refreshed and rejuvenated. I felt sharper and more tuned in to the lecture. I was loosening up around classmates, letting my personality shine through. I had so embraced my role as a runner that I had all but forgotten my goal of losing weight.

Eventually, I was recruiting others to join our morning runs. I became the one knocking on people's doors. While leading the group in a quick prerun stretch, I'd sometimes catch a look from Gene. A half smile, a hint of pride.

Not once did Gene and I pay attention to our times. We never clocked my speed. Each morning workout took a gentle eraser to the line between work and play until I could no longer tell the difference. I know now that I was in a state of leela.

On the last night of camp, I pulled out the formal clothes I had brought along for the next day's graduation ceremony. A pair of nice pants and a button-down shirt.

When I put on the pants, I immediately felt something was off. It seemed like I was stepping into a garbage bag. *Oh no*, I thought. *I must have grabbed Dad's by accident.*

When I looked at the label, I was stunned to find that the pants belonged to me. I pulled them up and they fell right off my waist.

How could this be possible? I hadn't noticed any type of bodily transformation. No one had said anything. But these pants had fit me snugly just months ago. I called my mom and asked her to bring me another pair.

The next morning, we met in the lobby of my dormitory. My parents had just finished their four-hour drive and my mom was holding the bag with my pants inside. When she saw me, that bag slipped out of her hand.

"Oh my god. You've lost so much weight," she said.

"It's not that much, Mom."

"So much!" she insisted.

Just then, my dad and uncle entered the lobby. My uncle took one look at me and exclaimed, "You look great, beta!" Then he turned to my dad and discreetly whispered in Hindi. "You told me it was a writing camp . . . not a fat camp."

I took the pants upstairs and got dressed. That graduation was the first time in my life that I could remember being truly proud of who I was and the way I looked.

Gene and I sat next to each other during the ceremony. Within a couple of hours, we would go back to our hometowns. Despite our best intentions, we never saw each other again. Gene went on to wrestle in college, becoming a star in his division. We lost touch soon after.

I never had the chance to thank Gene for what he did for me. The phone number I had for him was no longer working, and I couldn't find him anywhere on social media.

So Gene, on the off chance that you're reading this now . . . thank you. On that first day of camp, you could have sat anywhere, but you chose the seat next to mine. Until that moment in my life, I never thought someone who looked like you would ever want to associate with someone who looked like me.

You became my friend, breaking every assumption I had. When I confided in you that I was ready for change, you didn't give me a pep talk. You didn't try to teach me a lesson. Instead, you helped me build a high-quality habit.

I can trace a clear line between who I am today and those six a.m. runs we used to take. They taught me that confidence and consistency are twin pillars. To appreciate the power of doing little things over and over again. That the lines between work and play are ours to draw, and also ours to erase.

When we got back to our house later that evening, Mom went to the kitchen and started to warm up dinner for everyone. I walked into my bedroom and threw my suitcase on the bed.

I looked at my walls with a different set of eyes than before. I had only been gone for eight weeks, but everything had changed. I had changed.

I threw on a T-shirt and a pair of shorts. And I went for a run.

CHAPTER SIX

SEVA

FORGET YOURSELF TO FIND YOURSELF

My grandmother grew up on the border of India and Pakistan, the daughter of a local school headmaster. To help her father unwind after work, my *nani* would sing one of his favorite devotional songs, what we call *bhajans*.

On this particular day, she chooses a passage from the Bhagavad Gita. Its message is clear: the road to your dharma will appear when you turn your attention from serving yourself to serving others. This selfless service is a quality that my ancestors called *Seva* (pronounced save-ah). Seva is the belief that the fire within you isn't sustained by what you get, but rather by what you give.

When Nani finishes singing, she looks up at my great-grandfather, eager for his approval. The headmaster gazes at her lovingly. "That's the song I'd like you to sing this Sunday."

Seeing the confusion on his daughter's face, the headmaster explains that a great leader will be visiting their tiny village. "Someone who truly embodies the spirit of seva."

When the day arrives, nearly everyone in the village gathers around the town's center. The headmaster uses his booming voice to quiet the crowd and explain that this visit isn't a social one. Large parts of India were starving to death, and this visitor had come here to raise money for food. "We might not be wealthy," said my great-grandfather. "But we have food and shelter, which is more than others. Let's give lovingly and selflessly."

That's when he brings Nani to the center of the circle. She nervously scans the crowd. After an encouraging nod from her father, Nani begins to sing.

At first, her voice is shaky. By the bhajan's second line, the trembles smooth out. From the corner of her eye, she catches a glance of the special guest. He looks old and thin, wearing glasses and white garb. He sits on the ground in a cross-legged position.

The crowd is engulfed by his aura. He's like a magnetic beam drawing and channeling their attention to the final lines of Nani's performance.

When she finishes, he pops up from his cross-legged position like a man half his age. He approaches Nani with his hands in prayer, exuding a mix of strength and warmth.

"That was a lovely song, child . . . my name is Mohandas," he says.

"They call me Gandhi."

◆ ◆ ◆

Whenever I talk about Gandhi with my students, I can detect hesitation in the room. People tend to see him as beyond reproach, too saintly to be relevant in today's world. After all, his nickname was the mahatma, "the great one."

They are surprised to learn that Gandhi spent most of his life failing at everything he attempted. He was painfully shy and a mediocre student.

Gandhi went into law but was quickly handicapped by a fear of public speaking. During one of his first cases, he became so nervous that his hands clammed up and sweat seeped through his suit jacket. Embarrassed and ashamed, he fled the courtroom and never returned.

From that point on, he was known inside Indian legal circles as a "briefless barrister," because no client would hire him.

So what happened? How did a man with low confidence, a tarnished reputation, and a deep-seated fear of public speaking rise to become the leader of one of the largest independence movements in history? By prioritizing seva above all else and making it the doorway into his own dharma.

Gandhi said, "The best way to find yourself is to lose yourself in the service of others."

When authentically practiced, seva purifies your effort and elevates your performance. Because when you remove the motivation of credit, you no longer subdivide your energy. The part of you that was worried about the reward is now actively focused on the work itself.

President Harry Truman realized the power of seva when he said, "It is amazing what you can accomplish if you do not care who gets the credit."

The irony of seva is that it asks you to deprioritize personal benefit, yet the people who practice selfless service are often showered with status and rewards. But you can't game the system. You can't reach the peak performance of seva by projecting a spirit of service while secretly wishing for credit.

Gandhi wore a loincloth and died with less than two dollars to his name. Yet, eighty years later, he's still credited for toppling the British Empire and influencing the American Civil Rights Movement, all without raising a fist, much less a weapon.

The more I dig into how great leaders, artists, athletes, and entrepreneurs reach the top, the more I realize that there wasn't just a *why* to their actions, but a *who*. There was almost always someone else they were acting for, leading for, or fighting for.

It's not that they didn't care about rewards, but top performers tend to see personal benefits as cheap fuel. Rewards will get you going, but they won't keep you going.

Durable power comes from service.

When Gandhi forgot himself, he found himself. When he turned his attention to others, he stopped his stuttering, built his confidence, and rallied a nation.

◆ ◆ ◆

On April 13, 1919, a peaceful crowd of Indians gathered in a picturesque garden in Amritsar, Punjab. People gave speeches about how and why the past three hundred years of British rule had been so devastating for the Indian people. When Britain began its takeover, India was one of the wealthiest countries in the world. Now it was a symbol of famine and deprivation. The crowd was peaceful. There was agreement and applause. There was even singing and prayer.

Suddenly and without warning, British troops surrounded the garden, closed off all escape paths, and opened fire.

The protesters raised their arms in surrender. Others clawed and climbed at the surrounding walls for a way out. The gunfire that day didn't stop until every single available weapon was out of ammunition. When the smoke cleared, over a thousand bodies lay dead in that garden.

The Amritsar Massacre became a galvanizing force inside India. The question was no longer whether the Indian people needed freedom, but how best to achieve it.

This is where Gandhi reemerges in our story.

During his courtroom days, Gandhi realized that his fear of public speaking didn't come from the way others looked at him, it came from the way he habitually examined himself. Instead of focusing on his client, he had been overly concerned with his own image.

Gandhi saw that when he could shift attention from himself to the person he was serving, it would tap him into a deeper source of fortitude and durability. With that one shift, the quivers in his voice steadied, disparaging comments from opposing counsel slid off his back, and interrogations from the judge became part of the charm of being an attorney.

By forgetting himself, Gandhi began to find himself. He began to walk with effortless confidence and speak from his heart. And by the 1920s, Gandhi had captured India's imagination and given millions hope for freedom from British rule. The entire nation waited in anticipation for his clarion call, for the big idea that would pave the way to revolution.

So people everywhere were shocked, and even appalled, when Gandhi announced his first major act of resistance would be a protest march against the taxation of *salt*.

What his critics didn't realize is that Gandhi had shifted his attention away from himself and toward the people he was trying to serve. While politicians pounded the table, Gandhi searched for an answer to two simple questions: *Who am I really serving?* and *What do they need?*

By deepening into this state of seva, Gandhi came to a crucial and unifying insight. Freedom had little meaning unless it was shared by *everyone*. And most Indians lived in rural settings, struggling to gather enough food for a meal. They were malnourished, and many were starving to death.

When Gandhi closed his eyes and put himself in "the poor man's struggle," he saw farmers in India's countryside collapsing into comas due to a lack of salt. "Next to air and water," Gandhi said, "salt is perhaps the greatest necessity of life." And yet the British made it illegal for an Indian to collect or produce salt. If you were caught doing so, you could be arrested or killed. Many were.

Gandhi announced that he would be marching 241 miles from Ahmedabad to Dandi, an oceanside town, where he would personally disobey the law and collect his own salt from the sea. He invited the entire nation to join him in this march.

Only seventy-nine people took him up on the offer.

A *TIME* magazine reporter covered the start of the march, describing Gandhi as a man with a "spindly frame" and "spidery loins." The article reported that by the end of the first day, Gandhi was "haggard and drooping" and that "not a single cheer resounded" in the villages the protesters passed.

But Gandhi wasn't there to impress the American media, or to appear like a hero in anyone's eyes. He had lost himself entirely in the service of others.

And poor people everywhere could feel it. As the procession pressed on, momentum began to build. At first, folks began to cheer Gandhi on from the side of the road. Eventually, these bystanders joined in. Villagers left their huts, fishermen tied up their boats, even politicians took trains from Bombay to join the pack.

By week three of the Salt March, the group had swelled from less than one hundred to over one hundred *thousand*. The procession started like a school marching band. Now it felt like an entire city on the move.

On April 4, 1930, the crowd took its final steps to the Arabian Sea. An eyewitness described Gandhi's body in that final stretch, not as haggard or tired, but "golden and transfigured in the light of morning." He seemed strong and lean, like an athlete, with a rapid walk that "made you see how urgent" his message must be.

When Gandhi reached the water, he scooped up a handful of salty mud with both hands and said, "With this, I am shaking the foundations of the British Empire."

With this single act of seva, he did. The next day, legions of people flocked to the seaside to harvest salt. Families boiled the mineral water by the sand. They inhaled fresh ocean air, sang bhajans of gratitude, and danced around bonfires to mark one of the nation's very first unified acts of independence.

In the following days, over sixty thousand salt-gatherers were arrested and beaten by British police. But the winds of change were unstoppable. It was a new beginning for India—and the beginning of the end for Britain's rule. Gandhi's first act of seva was complete, proving what is possible when you turn your attention away from yourself and toward the service of others.

TIME, the same publication that mocked Gandhi's appearance in the early stages of the march, named him their "Man of the Year." He was invited to take an all-expenses paid trip to the United States to meet with dignitaries from around the world.

Gandhi passed. Instead, he sat on a dirt floor next to his spinning wheel and pondered his next act of seva.

RITUAL: THE SPOTLIGHT SWITCH

One of the simplest ways to engage in service is through a practice I call the *Spotlight Switch*.

Whenever you have to present a project or idea to a group, large or small, it can feel like the spotlight is pointed straight at you. And that can be pressure-filled and anxiety-inducing. With the spotlight switch, you deliberately shift that attention from yourself to the people you're serving. You make it about *them*.

One opportunity for the spotlight switch is a job interview. As an applicant, you would ordinarily be championing yourself— your work, your experience, your story. But what if, instead, you saw yourself as an advocate for the team you'd be joining? If, to prepare for the interview, you went deep into who the members of the team are and how they work?

You read their blog posts, watch any videos they've published, maybe even interview a couple of them about their experiences. As a result, you start to feel both an intellectual and emotional understanding of what's happening on the ground. By the time you walk into the room, you're way deeper than a job description. You have a résumé in hand, but the team is on your mind. You've moved from "How do I get the job?" to "How do I serve?"

The spotlight has shifted, which means it's no longer burning brightly on you. You're no longer inside your own head. You're free to speak with confidence and clarity. Because your purpose is pure.

THE DRUM MAJOR INSTINCT

Practicing seva doesn't mean you're putting yourself down or reducing yourself to a status beneath others. You can serve without taking on the identity of a servant.

Dr. Martin Luther King had studied Gandhi's spirit of seva and was now spending each day losing himself in the service of others. His acts of seva made him the face of the Civil Rights Movement, gained him the attention of presidents and prime ministers, and turned him into a figure of worldwide prominence.

Yet there was one speech that Dr. King delivered late in his career that seemed to go unnoticed by the masses. It wasn't given to an enormous crowd but rather a tiny congregation gathered in King's local church.

In front of familiar faces, Dr. King said that we all have a desire to lead the parade—a need for attention, a desire to be out front, a push to be first. King says that this "drum major instinct" is a natural part of who we are, and that each of us was born a little bundle of ego. "Our first cry was a bid for attention."

So it's unsurprising, King says, that we carry this primal need to achieve distinction into adulthood.

At this point, the members of Dr. King's congregation seem to be expecting him to admonish the drum major instinct. To tell them never to attempt to surpass others.

King says the opposite; he urges them to *protect* their drum major instinct. To not let go of wanting to lead, of wanting to be out front.

King tells his congregation that there is no doubt that the drum major instinct can be abused for self-service. But it can also be harnessed as a powerful and important source of good. There is nothing wrong with wanting to stand out so long as that distinction was in service to others.

Up until that moment, many in the church saw ambition as a flaw, not a feature. They viewed an appetite for greatness as almost an enemy to a life of service. And yet, here was Dr. King, a model of seva, telling them that the push for greatness and the pull to service weren't opposites, but complements. Dr. King tells his audience to preserve that feeling of wanting to be first. But to be first in moral excellence. To be first in generosity. To be first in *service*.

RITUAL: FROM GET TO GIVE

Dr. King told us not to shy away from wanting to be the best. But don't be the best at getting. Be the very best at giving.

Years ago, I discovered that the actor Bryan Cranston fell into a philosophy that closely matched the drum major instinct. Like Gandhi, Cranston had chosen a field that required presence and confidence, and like the young mahatma, he didn't have it. For most of his life, Cranston said he was "introverted" and "unsure of himself." As a result, he spent the first twenty years of his career going from audition to audition, while never landing the big role.

That's when Cranston met a coach named Breck Costin. A former actor himself, Costin had shifted his spotlight to helping other actors struggling to break out. Costin introduced Cranston to a new way of thinking about auditions. He convinced Cranston to view each tryout as an opportunity not to get something, but to give something away.

"When I audition, I'm not trying to get a job, but to give them something, my acting. The victory is not 'Did I beat that other guy out?' but 'Did I present that character as believably as I could?'"

This wasn't to protect Cranston's ego. It was to find himself as an actor—by losing himself in the service of others. By giving his gift away over and over again, Cranston found his confidence and resilience rising to a new level.

In a "get" model, it only matters whether you win or lose. In a "give" model, each audition (whether successful or not) meets the goal. Eventually, he got something in return. Cranston landed his first marquee role, playing the dad in *Malcolm in the Middle*. This led to him being cast as the character that made him a household name, Walter White in *Breaking Bad*.

To find yourself, forget yourself. Switch the spotlight and shift from getting to giving. This isn't a life hack, but a way of life.

♦ ♦ ♦

Mrs. Knauer announced we would be doing something a little different today. She rolled a television set into our seventh-grade classroom and popped in a VHS tape recording of Dr. Martin Luther King's "I Have a Dream" speech.

She paused King's address intermittently to make sure we were fully absorbing the gravity of the situation. How 250,000 people—five hundred times the size of our school—had gathered in one place to hear King articulate a vision for freedom.

I am spellbound by King's words, but what Mrs. Knauer shows us next stuns me. Up on the wall, she projects a luminescent photo of Dr. Martin Luther King inside his office. He has a resolute, determined look on his face. My attention, however, is focused entirely on the single photo hanging on the wall behind Dr. King's right shoulder.

It's a portrait of Mahatma Gandhi.

I squint to make sure that what I'm seeing is real. Gandhi was a huge figure in my home, but he had never been mentioned inside my classroom.

Until that moment, I had never discussed anything Indian at school. My two identities were separate. Indian boy and American child. My mornings at home were ensconced with statues of Ganesh while my school day kicked off with the American flag and Pledge of Allegiance.

I did whatever I could to fit in. I shielded my jacket from the smell of Mom's cooking. I wore BORN IN THE USA Springsteen T-shirts. More than once, I caked baby powder onto my skin to make it look whiter.

That morning in Mrs. Knauer's class, things began to change. I was staring at a photo of a great American hero, and behind his shoulder was a portrait of an Indian icon. For the first time, my two identities—Indian kid and American child—weren't at battle. They were in harmony.

A tiny voice whispered, *You don't have to be ashamed anymore.*

When the bell rang at the end of class, I couldn't get out of my seat. I just stared at the image of the reverend with the mahatma. While wiping the chalkboard, my teacher gave me a warm and knowing look.

As the hallways bustled with action, Mrs. Knauer pulled up a seat next to me. We talked about these two heroes, and how they built on each other's legacies. I asked her how these leaders became such great communicators. And that's when she said three simple words that changed my life.

"They had help."

She explained to me that great orators often collaborated with others. Martin Luther King had help writing his speeches, and so did Gandhi.

I biked home as fast as I could that day. When I burst through the door, I told my grandmother that the photo of Gandhi she had hanging in her room made an appearance on my school's slide projector. Then I proudly announced that I wanted to be a speechwriter when I grew up.

I wasn't sure what Nani's reaction would be. I wasn't telling her I wanted to be a doctor, a lawyer, or an engineer. If she was disappointed, she hid it well.

Nani had spent most of her life as a refugee and an immigrant. Around her neck, she wore a key to the happy home she was forced to flee when violence had engulfed her village in 1947.

Mom had told me stories about how Nani sang for Mahatma Gandhi when she was my age. Somehow, I'd never asked her about it. I always figured that I had time to hear the story later.

Nani told me that if I really wanted to be a speechwriter, I should just "go and do it now."

No, no, I explained. I wanted this to be my "career." I wanted to write speeches when I grew up. I had so many questions. Where do I need to go to school? What do I need to learn? What jobs do I need to get for someone to hire me in such a role?

Nani patiently listened to my monologue. Then she asked, "Who do you want to write speeches for?"

"Leaders," I answered, conjuring up images in my mind of

King and Gandhi leading revolutions, millions of people inspired by their words.

Breaking my daydream, Nani asked: "Aren't there leaders in this city? Such as elected officials?"

"Uh, yeah, I guess so."

"Then write speeches for them."

I laughed. "Nani, I'm a kid. They don't care about what I write."

"Do you want to write speeches?" she asked.

"Yes," I said.

"Then go write. Go sit at your desk and write a speech for someone."

So I did.

I settled on writing a speech for my local congressman, a guy by the name of Joe Knollenberg. Joe had no idea who I was, and I didn't know much about him. My dad kept a stack of old newspapers, which he used to stoke the fireplace in the winter. I sifted through those and found an article about Knollenberg's upcoming election, which was now only a few weeks away.

I pulled out a piece of looseleaf paper and in elementary-school style wrote my name and the date in the top right corner . . . in cursive. Then on the heading of the page I wrote in big wavy letters: "'Why You Should Re-Elect Me' by Joe Knollenberg."

I honestly don't remember what went on that page. I do remember that within a half hour of starting the speech, I was already pedaling my bike to Knollenberg's office, located in a strip mall down the road. Inside my back pocket was the persuasive prose key to his reelection.

People inside Knollenberg's office watched as I kicked my bike stand into place. I walked in excitedly and was greeted by a cheerful college intern. I asked if Congressman Knollenberg was in.

"He's in Washington right now. How can I help?"

Disappointed that Joe wasn't going to immediately read my speech, I pulled it out of my pocket and handed it to the intern. As he unfolded the paper, I explained what I had just done. He looked at me, then glanced at my work. I noticed he was no longer so chipper.

The intern stared at my speech. One page, single side, double spaced. Had he decided to read it out loud, it would have taken him a maximum of forty-five seconds.

The intern cleared his throat.

"Look . . . kid," he began. "The congressman has a couple of people in DC who write his speeches, but they're part of his senior staff. I don't even get to write his speeches."

I searched for the right words, but nothing came out. I tried to ask myself some version of *What would Gandhi or MLK do in a situation like this?* But I didn't find any answers. I was crushed.

The intern attempted to brighten the mood. "But, hey, the election is right around the corner and we need a lot of help stuffing envelopes."

Four hours later, I left the office with tiny little paper cuts on my thumbs from folding and stuffing literature.

On my dusky bike ride home, I seethed at Nani. When I stormed into the house, I started right in with her.

"You told me I could write speeches!" I recounted what happened, tears running down my cheeks. She listened and gave me a few moments to cry it out. Then she put her hand on my shoulder.

"Get some sleep," she said. "Then write another speech tomorrow."

"What? Didn't you hear what happened? No one wants my writing."

"Did you write today?" she asked.

"Yes," I said defeatedly.

"So do it again," Nani said. "You don't need anyone's permission to sit down and write."

There's a moment when you truly begin to understand how the people who raised you saw the world. Nani led her family through war and lifted them out of poverty. Yet, to her, an extraordinary life wasn't built through large, sweeping actions, but through lots of little acts. As long as those acts were in the spirit of seva, of service to someone or something, then they would eventually add up to something meaningful.

That night I lay in my bedroom, replaying what had happened inside the congressman's office. I hadn't received any kind of credit for the speech I'd written, but Nani was right . . . I had written a speech. My *first* speech.

If the spotlight was on me, then there was no next step. I had tried and failed. If the spotlight was on them, the people I was writing for, then the next step was clear. I needed to write another speech.

Some kids played sports after school, others played instruments. I wrote speeches. Most days I'd come home, grab a snack, sit down at the kitchen table, and pull out a few sheets of looseleaf paper.

I wrote speeches for people I admired, living or dead. I wrote for leaders in the East, like Mother Teresa, Nelson Mandela, and the Dalai Lama. I wrote for people in the West like Eleanor Roosevelt, Bobby Kennedy, and Cesar Chavez.

To write a speech for someone, you need to understand their story and also their voice. So I read the works of my heroes, gaining a deeper understanding of who they were and what they stood for. The spotlight was on them.

Speeches became my tool for service. My way to be a drum major, even if there was no band following me. I wrote speeches for anyone who asked, didn't matter the occasion. I wrote a Diwali celebration speech for an uncle, an anniversary speech for a cousin, and a retirement speech for my dad. I didn't graduate valedictorian, but I wrote the speech for the guy who did.

Throughout high school, I'd still visit Mrs. Knauer for feedback on my writing. The classroom was unchanged, her desk decorated with little bits of history—a bust of Frederick Douglass, a mini replica of Betsy Ross's original star-spangled banner, the same slide projector that transmitted the photo of King and Gandhi.

Side by side, Mrs. Knauer and I would sit at her small table and edit my speech. She'd make crisp little notes in the margins, always explaining each comment with care. We would audibly read each line. "Your ears are wonderful editors," she'd say.

At school, I had Mrs. Knauer. At home, I had Nani. Looking back now, I know it was these two powerful women who brought my dual identities—Indian kid and American child—together.

When I heard Mrs. Knauer was retiring, I visited her for one last editing session. That afternoon, we sat together, wrote together, and read together. After reciting a paragraph that I had reworked multiple times, she removed her glasses and drew a tissue from the tissue box. "This is you," she said. "This is your calling."

I raced my bike home that day, eager to start on my next speech. When I entered the kitchen, I found Nani sitting at the table, quietly humming a bhajan.

I decided then to finally ask my grandmother a question I should have asked long ago:

"What did you sing for Gandhi?"

Nani guided me to the floor of the living room. We sat down cross-legged on the ground, like she had as a little girl with her father.

And she began to sing.

CHAPTER SEVEN

TULA

LETTING GO AND TAKING CHARGE

As an Indian kid growing up in America, I often felt torn between two competing philosophies. Inside our temple, I learned the importance of letting go and surrendering to the flow of life. Outside the temple, I was taught to take charge and grab life by the horns.

Truthfully, neither seemed perfect. Western control sometimes felt like a recipe for stress and anxiety, while Eastern surrender hardly seemed like a formula for success.

It took me a long time to realize that these two philosophies—control and surrender—complement each other like a sailboat and the wind.

The art of bringing control and surrender into harmony is what my ancestors called *Tula* (pronounced too-lah). You can think of tula as "balance," or more precisely, "to put on an equal level." You're not elevating surrender over control or vice versa, but rather seeing both as essential to your dharma.

Anthony de Mello, a Jesuit priest and a psychotherapist, would recite a Sufi saying that nicely sums up tula: "Trust Allah but tie up your horse."

De Mello shared the parable of an elderly man who prayed he'd win the lottery. The old man would say, "God, I have been a devout worshiper. Now I'm old and I need some help. Let me win the lottery . . . it will help me in my old age." He prayed and prayed for months with no luck.

After three years, the man screamed out loud, "God give me a break!" God finally responded, "Give yourself a break . . . buy a ticket!"

With tula, you're not just sitting there and praying that something will happen. At the same time, you're tuned in enough to what's *already* happening so that you can be moved by natural currents. This can only happen through a careful partnership of control and surrender.

Gandhi's Salt March was not just an act of seva, it was also an act of tula. It was a perfect mix of taking charge and letting go—just enough effort at just the right time—and it changed history.

My grandfather was an embodiment of tula. Bauji was deliberate with his time, and yet always open to the potential of a moment. He was loosely structured throughout his days, tuning in to where he was needed. Watching him work was like watching a skilled sailboat captain.

Neither Gandhi nor Bauji surrendered themselves *entirely* to a higher power. They also never believed that they were acting alone. There was a wind available for them to harness, and it was always important to know which way it was blowing. To never oppose that natural force, and always use it to their advantage through timing and trust.

The longer you're on the path of your dharma, the more visible this power becomes. Great artists and athletes often talk about how their finest performances didn't just come from them, but "through them." They marvel at moments when they put in less effort and reached greater heights.

These moments are tula sweet spots. They live at the inter-section of control and surrender—where making things happen meets letting things happen. The purpose of this chapter is to help you find that balance.

THE MAGIC OF A MISSED GOAL

Simu Liu spent his entire life preparing to be an accountant. Money was always tight in the house and his immigrant parents pushed him hard to excel at school. Liu says the threat of poverty was too great for his parents to risk taking their foot off the gas.

Liu walked the path his parents had paved for him. He scored high marks, was accepted into a prestigious business school, graduated with honors, and was hired into a top accounting firm.

A few weeks into the job, Liu started to feel like it wasn't for him. He knew, deep down, that this expression had little to do with his essence. But he ignored those sensations and tried to focus on the work. After all, his education was already complete, the investment had already been made, and he had finally gotten his parents' approval.

Then on April 12, 2012, winds blew directly against Liu's mainsail. That morning he was tapped on the shoulder and led into the office of the managing partner. The boss informed Liu that he was being terminated "effective immediately" for under-performance.

Liu was escorted by security back to his desk where he was told to pack his things. As he placed his belongings into a small cardboard box, tears of humiliation welled up in his eyes. Moments later, Liu found himself walking the streets of Toronto trying to make sense of what had just happened.

Liu truly believed that his life was over. That night he was overcome with feelings of guilt and shame. The thought of breaking the news to his parents made him contemplate jumping off his balcony. But Liu didn't jump. Instead, he pulled out his laptop and searched Craigslist for job openings. His goal was to have something in hand when he told his parents he'd been fired.

One unusual posting caught his eye, and it had nothing to do with accounting or finance. A Guillermo del Toro film was looking for extras. On an impulse, Liu applied. He got the job.

As a child, Liu had been in love with movies and dreamed of becoming an actor. And for those few days on set, Liu believed he was reconnecting with his essence. He could feel the winds blow him back in the direction of his dharma.

He scoured Craigslist for more acting gigs, applying and auditioning for everything available. For the next five years, Liu found himself in a number of small, supporting roles on television shows and commercials. He wasn't making anywhere near the kind of money he did at his firm. But Liu was finally setting goals based on what mattered to him, not his parents.

Liu was putting in the effort, while also allowing his sails to harness the winds that were naturally nudging him further and further into acting. When he closed his eyes and tuned in to the forces surrounding him, he began to imagine the possibility of an Asian superhero on the big screen.

For years, cinemas had screened an endless array of superhero movies, yet none of these blockbusters were led by an Asian. Liu believed his dharma was to be the first.

So he invested his own money into creating a short film starring himself as a superhero. Liu's idea didn't get any traction in Hollywood, but it did put him on the radar of Marvel Studios.

When the studio later announced that it would be creating its first film with an Asian lead, Liu seized the moment and tweeted: "OK @Marvel, are we gonna talk or what?"

A few months later, Simu Liu was cast as the lead in *Shang-Chi and the Legend of the Ten Rings*.

I know, I know. Not everything turns out to be a Hollywood ending. But remember that until Simu Liu was fired from his job, his goal in life was to be a successful accountant. Applying for that posting on Craigslist wasn't simply an act of control, but an act of surrender. He was exerting effort, while also tuning in to a mysterious wind that seemed to be pushing him in a different direction. At a low point, Simu Liu caught a glimpse of his own dharma. And only then did he begin to believe that what was happening *to* him may have actually been happening *for* him.

RITUAL: KINTSUGI FOR YOUR HEART

In fifteenth-century Japan, shogun Ashikaga Yoshimasa accidentally dropped his favorite tea bowl, shattering it into small pieces. Devastated, he sent it to a repair shop.

When Yoshimasa received his prized possession back, he was horrified to find that the pieces had been stapled together. The bowl was functional again, but the parts were now joined with ugly metal brackets.

In a last-ditch effort, Yoshimasa asked a local artist to come up with a solution that would return the bowl to its natural beauty. When the artist brought it back to Yoshimasa, the cracks were no longer hidden or stapled.

Instead, they were highlighted with a visible golden lacquer. Lovely minerals now branched through the bowl like the stems of a beautiful plant.

The shogun was so delighted by the result that word of this new technique spread throughout the land. Eventually, it expanded into an art form and a philosophy called *Kintsugi* (pronounced kin-sue-gee), which means "golden repair." Kintsugi came to stand for celebrating the beauty of brokenness in art and in life. Because embracing imperfection can lead to something even more beautiful.

Have you ever heard the word *pronoia?* It's the opposite of paranoia. Whereas paranoia is the belief that the world is conspiring *against* you, pronoia is the feeling that the world is conspiring *for* you.

Pronoia is the foundation of kintsugi, because instead of resisting the cracks, you acknowledge, accept, and even embrace them—because you believe that the brokenness of the moment is leading to something stronger and more beautiful down the line.

Psychologists sometimes refer to this effect as "post-traumatic growth." Whereas resilience is the ability to bounce back from a negative event, post-traumatic growth is the ability to *develop* from it, to come back even stronger. The difference between resilience and growth depends almost entirely on how you treat yourself when things go wrong.

The next time something harmful happens, try practicing what I call "kintsugi for your heart." Instead of quickly stapling the pieces back together and moving on, take enough time to trace your fingers over the broken parts. Examine them with compassion and curiosity and explore the wisdom they offer. With patience, lacquer the pieces back together, proudly wearing those seams like a warrior wears their scars.

THE 85 PERCENT RULE

Ever since Mrs. Knauer showed us Dr. King's speech, I dreamed of delivering my own speeches on a big stage. After years of teaching inside classrooms and giving talks to smaller audiences, I finally got my chance. I started receiving invitations to address rooms of a thousand people or more. I was used to speaking to fifty people or fewer. This was a whole new ball game.

There were some basic things I needed to learn: how to project my voice, how to make eye contact from afar, and how to moderate a Q&A with a large crowd.

But learning all this didn't get me any closer to overcoming my biggest obstacle—the fear of messing up onstage. In smaller rooms, I could easily lose my train of thought, crack a joke about it, and get back on track.

On the big stage, it was different. I had a bright light shining on me, while the audience was in the dark. If I made a mistake, I'd be staring out at thousands of faceless silhouettes.

I had a classic case of performance anxiety. When I got in

front of large crowds, my throat tightened, my voice cracked, and my hands trembled.

So I took a different approach. Instead of leaving anything for chance, I wrote out my speech, word for word, and took those pages up with me to the podium. Rather than moving around the stage as I would inside a classroom, I simply stood behind the lectern and read my speech out loud.

The podium became my cocoon, shielding me from the risk of embarrassment. Behind the lectern, my voice no longer cracked, and my hands no longer shook. And yet, my speeches became dull and rehearsed. When these talks ended, people would clap politely. But I could tell they were uninspired. Unmoved.

I felt trapped between two bad options.

If I stayed behind the podium, I was in control, but my delivery was dull.

If I left the podium, I risked clamming up in front of a large crowd.

So I began turning down invitations to speak at large events. I told myself that I just wasn't made for the big stage—that I should stick to smaller audiences.

Then one day I heard a story about Carl Lewis, the Olympic sprinter who won an astonishing nine gold medals and set world records for the hundred-meter dash.

Lewis was what the racing world called a "slow starter." He would begin his races at the back of the pack but often ended up finishing first. A sprint coach studied Lewis's techniques and realized that he would start each race with a relaxed posture and maintain that stance the entire time.

In the final stretch, other runners would often tense up. Their faces would scrunch, their jaws would tighten, and their fists would clench. This would sap their energy, and Lewis would whoosh past them one by one.

Lewis's style became known in the running world and beyond as "the 85 percent rule." Instead of applying maximum effort, you're allowing yourself to remain loose, which frees up the awareness, presence, and power that is often associated with big wins.

We've been conditioned to believe that nothing good comes without maximum pressure. But that mindset has been debunked, and not just in sports. A comprehensive study out of City University in London looked at the career trajectories of nearly fifty-two thousand employees from a variety of industries.

Doctors Argyro Avgoustaki and Hans Frankort were surprised to find that extra effort—measured by hours and intensity—"did not predict any positive outcomes for employees." In fact, overtime work and extra intensity often *reduced* the quality of the output.

I began to reflect on what the 85 percent rule would look like for public speaking. What would it be like to reduce my intensity onstage by 15 percent? The answer came quickly. I had to let go of my overwhelming desire to make the crowd love me.

I would often fantasize about finishing my last words and watching the crowd leap to their feet with applause. It was a lovely dream, but it messed with my head. Every time I missed a beat or messed up a line, there was a voice inside saying, *There goes your standing ovation.* The extra pressure wasn't serving me—it was taking me out of the moment and weakening my performance.

So I decided to give the 85 percent rule a shot. My typical routine before a speech was to scan through my notes and re-rehearse my lines. Instead, I found a quiet spot backstage and softly whispered the word *easy* to myself over and over again.

By the time I got up onstage, I felt looser and more relaxed.

I wanted to deliver a strong speech, but I no longer felt the need to bring the house down. Before I knew it, I naturally walked out from behind the podium, leaving my notes behind.

There were times when I lost my train of thought—the nightmare scenario I had been trying to avoid in the first place.

But I found the 85 percent rule even more useful in those moments. When I made a mistake, my original instinct was to apply *more* effort. Now I allowed myself to apply less. I would take a quick beat, let my hands soften, and create a little space to rebound. Then I'd move on.

With each speech, I found myself surrendering more and more to the stage. I was prepared, yet present. I was committed, but loose. Little by little, I was feeling my way into the balance of tula.

My audiences noticed. When the lights came back on, their faces were different. They were excited and energized. There were more questions during Q&A. And after a couple of months, I finally received my first standing ovation.

THE TRUST OF TULSI

In August 1947, Gandhi's dream of an independent India finally came true. Before the British made their exit, however, they divided the subcontinent into two separate states—Muslim-majority Pakistan and Hindu-majority India. In between these borders was a disputed territory, and by October, a bloody war had broken out. Hindus were chasing Muslims out of India and Muslims were chasing Hindus out of Pakistan.

My mom and her family were among those who suddenly found themselves living in a country where they were no longer welcome. She was only five years old when Nani woke her in the middle of the night to tell her they had to flee their home. The violence on the streets of Karachi was too close. Nani locked the house behind them and then placed the key on a string around her neck, hoping that one day they would return.

Everyone from my family fled to the nearest refugee camp that night. Everyone except for my great-uncle Tulsi (pronounced Thul-see).

It's hard not to look at a photo of Tulsi and smile. His eyes are dark brown and daring. His hair is presentable but wild enough to assert its freedom. And his grin—it's almost as if he and the camera were together on an inside joke.

Tulsi was an entrepreneur and a risk-taker. When he was in his early twenties, he opened a local grocery store at a prime intersection with lots of foot traffic. Some of my mom's earliest memories are from inside that store, where the entire family worked shifts at one time or another.

Tulsi spent years building it into a successful business. Every penny he had was tied up in that store. He couldn't fathom the idea of walking away with nothing. He was forcefully determined to make the best of a bad situation.

Tulsi knew that when the mobs reached his town, their intent would be to torch its Hindu-owned homes and shops. Tulsi had an insurance policy that covered fires. If he stuck around until the mob burned down his store, he could file a claim. The payout from that claim would be enough to give his family a chance to start a new life.

Tulsi's family thought his scheme was insane. When the mob came to burn down the store, they would also kill Tulsi. No matter the reward, the risk was too great. They begged

Tulsi to join them. But nothing his family or friends said could change his mind. He ignored the way the winds were blowing and hoped that through sheer force of will, he could achieve his desired outcome.

For the next few days, Tulsi kept his shop open, selling goods to the few customers who remained. It didn't take long for the violence to reach his streets, though, at which point even the hold-outs fled.

But Tulsi settled in. After all, everything was going according to plan.

And then, a stranger strolled into the store. He wore a long white robe and a skullcap. His dark brown eyes scanned the store and eventually met Tulsi's line of sight.

My Hindu uncle and this Muslim man stared at each other in silence. Neither made a move, but both understood what was at stake. The war was now raging on the streets outside, and they both seemed to wonder if it was their duty to continue it inside.

Finally, the stranger broke the silence. "What are you still doing here?"

Tulsi gave the man a smile. "This shop is all I have."

The stranger nodded knowingly. It turned out he, too, owned a small store on the other side of the India-Pakistan border, in Bangalore. He, too, had fled his home due to violence.

With so much in common, and in such a heightened situation, the two men forged a quick bond. The stranger warned Tulsi, "Your shop is about to be burned down. I'm surprised it hasn't been already."

"That's what I'm waiting for," replied Tulsi. "If someone else burns it down, then I'll have a chance at collecting the insurance money."

"But they'll kill you, too," the stranger said.

That's when inspiration struck my great-uncle. He looked the stranger in the eyes, and asked, "Will you burn my shop down?"

The man chuckled, charmed by Tulsi's earnest nature. The stranger then reached for a key tied to a string around his neck. "I can do better than that," he said. "This is the key to my shop back home. Let's switch. I'll give you mine and you give me yours."

Tulsi's initial impulse was to say no, to further dig in his heels. He had come so far, was he really going to abandon his plan now? Maybe the stranger's key opened a real shop or maybe it unlocked a local latrine. Even if there was a store, Tulsi had no idea if it was still standing, if it had survived the riots.

But something stopped Tulsi from rejecting the stranger's offer. Something made him see that he had been too rigid in his beliefs. He'd been clinging too stubbornly to his plan, closing himself off from other possibilities. He had been all force and no trust.

This stranger blowing into his store felt like more than a coincidence. It was a strong gust of wind moving him in a new direction. The universe was telling him it was time to reduce his effort, harness these winds, and trust that they would lead him to a better place.

Tulsi pulled out his key and placed it on the counter. The stranger did the same. They embraced and wished each other luck.

The moment Tulsi left his store, he became a refugee, on the run. Making his way to the newly formed India was now an even more perilous task than it was when his family had fled. Danger was lurking around every corner. But Tulsi managed to smuggle himself onto a ship and then hop a train straight to Bangalore, to the coordinates he'd been given by the stranger.

After days of hard travel, a weary, hungry Tulsi approached a tiny locked-up shop. While other stores on the street had been looted and burned, this one looked untouched.

Tulsi pulled the metal skeleton-shaped key out of his pocket and inserted it into the casing above the doorknob. He immediately felt a little click in his hand. He turned, and the door sprang open.

It was dark when Tulsi entered his new store. He pulled out a match and lit a kerosene lamp sitting on one of the counters. As Tulsi scanned the aisles, he found military-style clothing— uniforms, T-shirts, flags, and banners. And there, against the back walls, were rolled-up carpets that my uncle recognized as Persian rugs. Each textile was handwoven with naturally dyed wool.

Tulsi ran his hands down the wefts in the carpet. They were genuine. These rugs alone were worth as much as his store back home.

My great-uncle Tulsi had hoped the stranger's shop would help pull his family out of poverty. But it would do much more than that. It would create ripple effects for generations to come and make possible the life I know now. Right there, Tulsi could see it; how his past, present, and future all came down to a single moment of tula. The power of it all brought him to his knees.

CHAPTER EIGHT

KRIYA

ACTION LEADS TO COURAGE

You've made it this far. You've learned how to discover and devote yourself to your dharma. Now, in our final chapter, we turn to the importance of *acting* on it.

The legendary dancer Martha Graham once said that what's inside of you can only be expressed through action. If you don't act, it will never exist in any other medium. Your essence will be lost forever.

Kriya (pronounced kree-ya) is the action you perform for the sake of your dharma. Without kriya, without deliberate action, your dharma slips from hope to regret.

Expressing your essence requires movement and participation. Plenty of philosophical books discuss the importance of "being." But dharma is action-oriented—it's about both being and doing. With kriya, you're doing from the depths of your being.

We've been conditioned to take action only if we're sure it will work. When you're about to walk through the doorway of your dharma, doubt often creeps in and whispers three crippling words: *I'm not ready.* I'm not ready to step into that role, to run with that idea, to speak my mind.

Before long, your calling seems more like a pipe dream. Imposter syndrome sets in. You feel like you're not good enough, deserving enough, young enough, or worthy enough for this dharma to be yours.

So what do we do? We wait. Instead of acting, we search for certainty. We go looking for evidence that we've got what it takes to bring our dharma to life.

Santiago Ramón y Cajal, widely considered the father of neuroscience, observed how people would "thrive on the thrill" of setting goals but crumbled when it was time to act. He believed that being ready was a choice, not a feeling. That if you choose to act, the feeling would follow.

That theory grew to what neuroscientists now call "behavioral activation." Through deliberate action, you can activate the feeling of readiness.

This is the lifeblood of kriya. Instead of waiting for courage to take action, you're taking action and letting courage catch up along the way.

◆ ◆ ◆

In 1960, Marian Wright Edelman was a senior at Spelman College. Feeling a strong pull toward the Civil Rights Movement, she had already joined marches and attended sit-ins. But she wanted to do more. She wanted to make fighting for justice her life's work. She just wasn't sure how.

Like so many others at the time, she looked to a preacher from Atlanta for answers.

When Dr. Martin Luther King came to Edelman's campus, she expected him to unfurl a map and share his step-by-step vision for the movement. She expected to find comfort in his confidence, courage, and certainty.

Edelman's expectations were shattered that day. Dr. King walked up to the podium like a man about to deliver a eulogy. He seemed weighed down by anxiety, doubt, and despair.

Dr. King didn't lay out a plan or a road map. Instead, he told the young and hopeful audience that he was unsure about what the future held.

You might imagine what a letdown this was for the activists inside that room. Their rights were pinned on a man who seemed overcome with uncertainty.

Yet the reverend made clear that doubt and action aren't opposites. That courage isn't the absence of fear, but the ability to pair doubt with action. Dr. King may not have had the answers, but he told his followers that certainty can never be a prerequisite for action.

"If you can't fly, then run. If you can't run, then walk. If you can't walk, then crawl. But whatever happens, keep moving forward."

Inspired by Dr. King, Edelman went to Mississippi to register Black voters. When she got to the Delta region, she saw unspeakable levels of poverty. Black people were starving due to laws that intentionally limited their access to food. Dharma was knocking at Edelman's door—and before doubt could muscle its way in, she took action.

Edelman began cold-calling journalists and policymakers. She convinced national leaders, including Senator Bobby Kennedy, to take a tour of the Delta and witness the suffering firsthand.

Edelman then founded the Poor People's Campaign, which set out to bring impoverished people from every corner of the country to Washington, DC. There, they would begin a massive, multiweek demonstration, putting the hardships of the poor on America's center stage.

Many doubted that Edelman could pull off such an ambitious undertaking. She had serious doubts herself. But Edelman had a secret weapon. She managed to convince Dr. King himself to come on board and lead the demonstrations in DC.

With Dr. King at the helm, Edelman had the kind of momentum that even her doubters could not deny. Leaders emerged from around the country to support the Poor People's Campaign, and Edelman entered the spotlight as a rising star.

Ever since she was a teenager, Edelman had felt a sacred duty, an inner necessity, to fight for the rights of her people and to protect society's most vulnerable. Now she was acting on that call and living her dharma.

But just before the Poor People's Campaign was set to launch, Dr. King was murdered.

Riots broke out everywhere—and as the country burned, Edelman's heart froze. She had lost her mentor and her greatest hope for a brighter future. Getting this campaign off the ground without Dr. King seemed like an impossible task. Doubt and despair grew from a whisper to a scream.

In the midst of everything falling apart, however, Edelman remembered an image of Dr. King. Not the memory of a man boldly leading marches in Montgomery, Alabama. Nor the recollection of him addressing 250,000 activists at the Lincoln Memorial.

She saw a young preacher, quietly speaking from a podium at

her college campus. A man filled with doubt, openly expressing the same sense of uncertainty and fear that she was feeling at this very moment.

That's when she fully understood something. Dr. King hadn't been successful because of his courage. He was successful because he took action, and let courage catch up along the way. If her mentor could be gripped by fear and still push forward, then so could she.

Edelman got back on her feet and committed herself to the Poor People's Campaign.

For forty-two dramatic days, Americans were confronted with faces of suffering that most did not even imagine possible in the United States. Politicians could no longer ignore the issues of hunger and poverty—they had now entered the public consciousness. Something had to be done.

Edelman's actions led to expanded food stamp access, free school lunch programs for impoverished children, and the creation of the Children's Defense Fund.

She became an inspiration to college students who, like her, wanted to continue the fight for civil rights. At podiums inside universities, Edelman would channel the same message she received in college from Dr. King.

Action leads to courage. "You don't have to see the whole staircase . . . just take the next step."

TWO-WAY DOORS

In his Nobel Prize–winning theory of "loss aversion," Daniel Kahneman demonstrated that the pain we feel from making a bad decision can be *twice* as powerful as the pleasure we receive from making a good one.

This gets to the heart of why acting on dharma can be so hard. We are often much more consumed with what can go wrong than what might go right. We do all that we can to reduce uncertainty. We conduct research, create schedules, seek advice—everything except the action itself.

Planning can sometimes make us feel like we're making progress when we're actually stuck in place. By the time we're ready to act, the moment may have already passed.

I was a little surprised to see this philosophical sentiment captured in a shareholder letter written by Jeff Bezos. Amazon was in its twentieth year in business and had gone from an unknown startup to one of the most valuable companies of all time. In his letter, Bezos credited that success to a willingness to act without certainty:

"Some decisions are consequential and irreversible or nearly irreversible—one-way doors—and these decisions must be made methodically, carefully, slowly, with great deliberation and consultation. If you walk through and don't like what you see on the other side, you can't get back to where you were before. But most decisions aren't like that. They are changeable, reversible—they're two-way doors. . . . You can reopen the door and go back through."*

As an entrepreneur who has both failed and succeeded, I am sometimes asked why I have such a high appetite for risk.

Here's the truth: I don't. I'm as afraid of failure as anyone else.

---

* Jeff Bezos, "Exhibit 99.1" U.S. Securities and Exchange Commission. https://www
.sec.gov/Archives/edgar/data/1018724/000119312516530910/d168744dex991.htm.

In fact, I often worry about running out of money and not being able to take care of my kids. Ask my wife, Leena. She'll tell you how every few months I freak out about finances.

This mindset doesn't make me an obvious candidate for entrepreneurship because startups are inherently risky. The reason I've been able to tolerate that fear is that I've come to see most risks as reversible. They're two-way doors.

The person who inspired me to finally start my own company didn't have a traditional success story. My friend Brian had been heavily into indie rock music since he was a kid. In his early thirties, he decided to leave a cushy job inside a top consulting firm to create a startup that would help indie bands become more easily discovered. He wasn't sure if it was going to work but felt compelled to try.

He pulled together a pitch deck, raised a little money from friends and family, hired a developer to help him build the service, and for the next two years, tried to create a working business model. But Brian wasn't able to gain enough traction to raise a new round of funding, so he shut the company down.

Why then did his story inspire me?

Because a few months after he failed, Brian was back to his job at the consulting firm. His decision to become an entrepreneur had been a two-way door.

At first, Brian felt ashamed. Like he was returning to his old role with his tail tucked between his legs. But he soon began receiving encouraging notes from coworkers. They'd heard about his startup venture and were curious about the experience, about how he decided to take the leap.

Suddenly, Brian was hosting lunches and coffees to share his story. That piqued the interest of some of the company's higher-ups. Many of the consulting firm's clients were big corporations that wanted to think and behave more like startups. They asked Brian to start joining senior leadership discussions about entrepreneurial thinking, a role that he would never have been asked to play in the past.

Within a year, Brian was put in charge of a brand-new team of consultants that helped large companies partner with small startups. It was as if the two major paths in his life had merged into one.

Even if he had simply returned to his previous position, Brian's story would have been a motivator for me. Before seeing his path unfold, I viewed entrepreneurship as a one-way door. I believed that failing would cause irreversible damage to my career.

However, I had just seen my friend walk through that door, fail, and come back. That's not to say I envied Brian's outcome. I wanted to succeed. But he made me realize that even a risky move like leaving a full-time job to start a company is a two-way door.

And that's what gave me the courage to try.

RITUAL: QUICKLY TEST THE HINGES

When a decision feels risky, and you're not sure whether to take action, here's a *very* simple test to help you decide. Ask yourself: *If I move forward, will I be able to come back? Will I be able to return to the job or life I had before?*

If the answer is no, then by all means spend time collecting data and seeking advice. Do whatever you need to do in order to reduce your risk.

If the answer is yes, then this is a two-way door. You can walk through, free from the need for complete certainty.

TINY CONTRACTS

Even though most actions are reversible, each one you take deserves your full commitment. Because if you don't fully commit to a choice—if you're one foot in and one foot out—how will you really know whether the action you took was right?

That's why a two-way door is best combined with what I call a tiny contract. This is a binding agreement you make with yourself to go all in on a course of action for a fixed period of time. The length of the contract is completely up to you—it could be a week, a month, or longer.

At the end of your tiny contract is a checkpoint where you shift from action mode to reflection mode.

This is when you should review your original decision and take stock of where it has led you. Until that checkpoint arrives—no matter the annoyances, distractions, or obstacles—your heart remains in the action.

Tiny contracts might sound like a way to avoid commitment, but they're actually a tool for strengthening it. Studies show that most of us approach our work only partially engaged because we're constantly scanning for better opportunities.

With a finite and focused commitment, you are less distracted by competing priorities. With a checkpoint in place, you are no longer dividing your energy between executing your decision and questioning whether it was the right one in the first place. When doubt rears its head, you can look it in the eyes and say, "I've scheduled time for us later."

You're not suppressing the part of you that wants to know what else is out there. You're being deliberate with your dharma—budgeting time to go all in, and also finding time to step back and reflect.

Years ago I was introduced to John, the CFO of a Fortune 500 manufacturing company. He had been with the same corporation for more than thirty years and had climbed all the way to the top from an entry-level role.

John was now in his late fifties and I asked him how much longer he planned to work for the company. His answer was "one year." I assumed that meant he was planning to retire in a year, but as it turns out, he was open to staying in the workforce for at least another five. He simply renews his commitment through one-year contracts.

Each summer, he and his wife take a personal retreat to their favorite spot on a secluded lake in Wisconsin. During the day, he'll sit out by the water, and allow nature to bring him a sense of peace. When he finally finds a place of stillness, he asks himself: *What do I love . . . and am I doing that?*

That week by the lake serves as the checkpoint for his one-year contract. If John still feels like he is in his dharma, finding joy in what he does, then he'll commit to another year.

John's employer has no idea that he spends a week each summer evaluating whether to leave. But these contracts aren't just for John's benefit, they're for the company's as well.

After making a decision to recommit for one more year, John returns with a vigor that energizes everyone around him. Things feel fresh again. He feels ownership over his choice to be there, because he's made a deliberate choice to stay. And he knows another checkpoint is always around the corner.

RITUAL: KNOWING WHAT YOU DON'T KNOW

In 1999, psychologists David Dunning and Justin Kruger published a research study that changed the way that we think about personal growth. Before the study, the common belief was that the more you know about a subject, the more confident you feel in your expertise.

But Dunning and Kruger demonstrated that the opposite can also be true. The more you know, the *less* confident you might feel.

For example, if you were to invest ten hours into learning a new computer programming language, you might expect to feel ten hours smarter. In reality, you could actually feel like you know less than before.

Why? Because during those ten hours, you also became more aware of all the things that you *don't* know. Your knowns increased, but so did your unknowns.

You've probably come across people who understand very little about a subject and yet come across as supremely confident. That's because they don't know what they don't know. They believe, sometimes sincerely, that they've mastered the topic.

It sounds counterintuitive, but sometimes we stop learning in order to feel smarter. In meetings, for example, we might decide against asking a clarifying question to protect our confidence.

The instinct to protect our own ego can be strong, but we must fight it in order to keep learning. When someone throws out an acronym that you've never heard before, don't be afraid to interrupt them for an explanation. Don't stop keeping up with the latest findings, research, and trends in your field, even if you believe that you're already an expert. Set a tiny contract to become a little more engaged, a little more informed every day. After a few months, you'll be surprised at the difference a couple of hours a week can make.

Living your dharma means living in search of a question, rather than resting in the comfort of an answer.

LIVE THE QUESTION

In *Letters to a Young Poet*, Rainer Maria Rilke writes to a young army cadet who is grappling with whether to stay in the military or pursue a career in writing. In one of those letters, Rilke tells the cadet to have patience with his unsolved problems and "live the questions themselves."

The young army cadet was looking for an answer, and instead Rilke told him to "live the question." Not to analyze the question. Not to ponder it, weigh it, or plan it—but to live it.

At only eighteen years of age, Dennis Rodman was homeless and living out of a garbage bag. With nowhere to go or be, he spent a lot of his time exploring the streets of Dallas, observing and asking questions about anything that interested him. Basketball was one of those things, so he'd often stop by the courts to watch a game in progress.

It was here that Rodman often found himself a victim of

bullies. They called him ugly and told him that, at five foot nine, he was too short to play. So he rarely did.

Instead, Rodman devoted his attention to a pinball machine inside the local 7-Eleven. He would get completely absorbed in the game. He loved anticipating where the ball would head—based on the speed of the release, the angle of the contact, and the curvature of the source. The "not-knowingness" of it all lit him up inside.

Rodman loved that pinball machine so much that he slept behind the 7-Eleven every night for a year. And over the course of that year, something mystical happened, something that sports commentators have since called an "act of God."

Dennis Rodman grew from five foot nine to six foot eight.

To put this into context, most human beings stop growing by the age of fifteen, and it's exceedingly rare for someone to get taller after the age of eighteen. When it does happen, it's usually by an inch or two, and the growth is typically the result of outstanding nutrition and sleep. Dennis Rodman grew nearly a foot while sleeping on the sidewalk and eating scraps.

With his new physical presence, Rodman headed back to the basketball courts. You can only imagine the look on the bullies' faces when supersized Rodman made his appearance. It's like a scene ripped out of a movie. Every bullied kid's dream.

Those courts became Rodman's new home. He played all day, every day, teaching himself the fundamentals that he never learned from a coach. He began to break the game down into components. And the component that really sparked his curiosity, the one that became the question he decided to live, was rebounding.

To Rodman, the court was one giant pinball machine. The rim was the metal flapper keeping the ball in play. Watching a ball ricochet off it transported him back to his time at the 7-Eleven. He found himself fascinated by the angles and arcs of a missed shot, the patterns, and endless possibilities.

That curiosity fueled his actions and behaviors. And in turn, those actions fueled his confidence on the court and powered him all the way to the NBA.

There's a story I love from my hometown of Detroit, where Dennis Rodman began his pro career. During practice one day, the Pistons' captain, Isiah Thomas, noticed that Rodman was standing on the sidelines just watching the rest of the team shoot balls.

Thomas marched straight up to Rodman and told him, "You have to participate; everybody's shooting layups, you have to shoot layups too."

Rodman responded, "I'm just watching the rotations on the basketball."

"Excuse me?" Thomas replied.

Rodman pointed to the rim. "When you shoot, your ball spins three times in the air. Joe's sometimes spins three and a half or four times."

Basketball legend Charles Barkley described rebounding as "just go get the damn ball." Rodman saw it as a science—dissecting it all with the enthusiasm of a PhD candidate.

Dennis Rodman was never a standout shooter, passer, or dribbler. Yet his fascination and commitment to rebounding made him one of the most confident players in all of pro sports. Even as his star rose, he continued to live the questions. He understood that the pursuit of an endless education gave him an edge. And that edge led him to five NBA championships and a spot in the Hall of Fame.

RITUAL: TO-LEARN INSTEAD OF TO-DO

A few years ago, I decided it was finally time for me to write my first book. As soon as I set that as a serious objective, my anxiety began to ratchet up. When I woke up each morning, I was stressed by the vast distance between me and the finish line. When I sat down at my desk, I felt tight and rigid. The anxiety pushed me to write—and yet most of what ended up on the page felt forced.

After reading Rilke's advice to live the question, I tried something new. I shifted my goal from "write a book" to "become a better writer." In other words, I transitioned my goal from a "to-do" into a "to-learn."

Now, this might seem like a minor adjustment, but the mental shift was huge. Almost immediately, the tension gave way to a much more joyful source of energy—my curiosity.

I became deeply interested in the habits of writers I admired. I studied their work, their commentaries, and their interviews. I set a tiny contract to write every single day for one year because I realized the only way to become a better writer is to actually write.

A lot of what I wrote ended up in the trash bin. But by living the question, I felt far more energized, entertained, and creative. There were very few days when I dreaded the work itself. In fact, I was so lit up by the "to-learn" experience that I began working on my second book as soon as I finished the first.

Society can condition us to believe that if you don't have a set of objectives that can ultimately be checked off a list you're floundering. You're without a sense of purpose and direction.

I don't think that's true.

Objectives signal an end, whereas questions point to a possibility. To-learns take you down a path that is nimble and resilient.

They allow you to discover what else is possible while moving you boldly in the direction of your dharma.

✦ ✦ ✦

A few months after my grandfather first introduced me to the concept of dharma, a young and energetic priest named Sastry moved from Calcutta to our local temple in Detroit.

Sastry's skin was a few shades darker than most of us, which made his already-vibrant smile even brighter. He was always dressed in a saffron-colored robe, with a mark of red powder on his forehead called a *tikka*.

The priest's voice was rich and deep, cutting through the noisiest of rooms. Even among hundreds of people chanting "Ommmmm," you could always place Sastry's voice inside the hall.

After the main prayer was finished, Sastry would pull me and the other kids into a semicircle and teach us the English interpretation of that day's sermon. I didn't realize it at the time, but Sastry was picking up right where Bauji had left off. And on one particular day, he imparted the most important dharma lesson of all.

Sastry asked us what we wanted to be when we grew up. Answers went off like popcorn from around the room. Teacher. Doctor. Actor. Firefighter. Power Forward for the Detroit Pistons.

Sastry's smile grew deeper and brighter. "Wonderful!" he exclaimed after each response. When we quieted down, Sastry leaned in and delivered his message.

"You can live your life with either a map or a compass."

Sastry explained that a map is focused on a destination and a set of step-by-step directions to reach that place. For those who said they wanted to be a doctor, the map was to get into a reputable college, get good grades, and go to medical school. A compass is different, said Sastry. It doesn't care as much about your final destination—it's only concerned with the *right next step*. Your compass doesn't follow a set of predetermined directions. Instead, it tunes in to where you are and where you truly want to go next.

"Most of us live our lives with a map," said Sastry. "Live yours with a compass."

Every kid in the room was surprised by Sastry's message. Was he really telling us *not* to have a life plan? To simply go wherever the road takes us? This was the opposite of what we were being taught by our immigrant parents.

One of the kids raised his hand. "Sastry . . . are you telling us not to have goals?"

The question elicited a laugh from the priest. "You should *absolutely* have goals in life. Goals give us energy . . . something to strive for." The room relaxed a bit. Sastry was back to speaking our parents' language. That's when he threw the final curveball:

"But also realize that you will change, even after those goals are set. Your interests will change, your relationships will change, your mindset will change."

Sastry's parting message that day was this: Your dharma is *fluid*, not fixed. Your essence was with you from the day you were born, but the way you *express* that essence can change over time.

When you decide to take action in life, take it *fully*. Be present and completely focused. But after the action is complete, always pull out your compass and decide the *right next step*. Because what you mapped out in the past may not always match what you want for your future.

Sastry's message was more than I could fully process as a kid. But decades later, when I fully realized my essence was to tell stories, Sastry's visual of the map and compass immediately came to mind. Instead of trying to draw out a comprehensive life plan as a storyteller, I needed to simply ask myself: *What is the right next step?*

I used the chisels we discussed in chapter 1 (Sukha) to create a dharma deck that consisted of five exciting ways I could express my essence as a storyteller: public speaking, podcasting, teaching, writing books, and making films.

But there was a sixth idea that kept calling to me: running for public office. It was something I had been interested in since the seventh grade. But that felt so far from my essence now that it never made the deck.

And then Donald Trump became the forty-fifth president of the United States. Overnight, it felt like the country had become a much angrier, more hostile place—particularly for anyone who wasn't white. As the father of two daughters, I was stunned, upset, and afraid for their future.

I became more aware of the Silicon Valley bubble I had put myself in and completely absorbed by the state of affairs in other parts of the country—particularly in Michigan. My home state had voted for every Democratic presidential candidate since 1992, but it had flipped to Trump in 2016. I wanted to know why.

I began taking frequent trips back home to Detroit. I spoke to neighbors who were registered Democrats who voted for Trump. I attended city council meetings, joined rallies, and spoke to union members. I did my best to leave my certainty at the door and live the questions.

As I learned more and more, my compass began to sharpen, and I felt inspired to take action. And not just from a distance, but on the ground. What started as a whisper in my head grew into a bold, clear voice—it was telling me to leave San Francisco, move back to my home district in Michigan, and run for Congress.

At first, the idea sounded so absurd that I simply waited for it to pass. Winning felt like too much of a long shot. And again, I couldn't see how becoming a political candidate aligned with my dharma. Yet every time I tried to dismiss the idea, I heard Sastry whispering in my ear: our dharma is never fixed, it's fluid. Your essence remains the same—the way you express that essence can change in unpredictable ways.

Running for public office was a childhood dream that I ditched long ago, yet here I was, feeling a deep and undeniable pull to take action. There were more first-time candidates running for office in 2018 than ever before. So I decided to stop listening to the voice inside my head that said *You're not ready* and started asking, *Why not me?* Even if it was a long shot, I'd be able to tell my daughters—when they were old enough—that I got in the ring and fought for what we believed in.

I moved back to Michigan and announced my candidacy to a local newspaper. Over the next year, I knocked on over a thousand doors in my hometown. This was a district that hadn't elected a Democrat in forty years and had never elected a person of color. Some slammed the door in my face, and others told me to "go back to my own country."

But the vast majority of people were kind and decent. We didn't always share the same worldview, but when we looked each other in the eyes and shared our stories, those differences seemed to matter less.

In those doorways, something occurred to me: running for office *was* connected to my essence as a storyteller. I was spending half my days listening to stories—and the other half sharing them. I was giving speeches, pitching donors, creating commercials, and honing my message.

This wasn't a detour from my dharma. I was fully in it.

This realization reenergized me at a time when I needed it most. It helped me find the extra gear that I believed would help take our campaign all the way. Running for office has a lot in common with running a startup. Everything is chaotic. You're operating on a bootstrapped budget, with a slim chance of success. The difference is that with elections there are no second chances, no soft landings, and no extensions. On Election Day, it's over. You've either won or you've lost.

And when the results came in on election night, I had lost. It was over for me.

The past year had been so all-consuming that I never took the time to consider what life would be like if I didn't win. My compass had only pointed me to my next step. And now I was back in suburban Detroit with zero job prospects and no idea where to take my career. Meanwhile, my friends back in San Francisco seemed to be thriving in theirs. I had taken a big swing for the sake of my dharma and fallen flat on my face. Instead of following my heart, I wished I had listened to the voice in my head that had said *You're not ready, this is all one big pipe dream.*

My life in Silicon Valley wasn't perfect, but I had built a name for myself there.

Now I feared that I had walked through a one-way door and left all that behind for good. I feared that chasing my dharma had been a big mistake.

Aware of my restlessness and anxiety, Leena started assigning me tasks to get me out of the house and take my mind off things.

That included escorting our daughters to their first dance class at the local temple—the same one I had attended as a kid.

I held my little girls' hands as we walked through the large carved-wood doors I had entered every Sunday as a child. We walked barefoot across the cold marble foyer and tucked our shoes into my old cubbyhole.

After dropping my kids off at dance, I went to the main prayer hall and sat down on the carpet. Then I did something I hadn't done in decades. I prayed.

When I closed my eyes, memories of Sastry came flooding back. His bright-white smile, the red tikka on his forehead, the majestic flow of his saffron-colored robe. In the background were the sounds and smells of my childhood. Chatter from the aunties preparing aromatic dishes for the after-service lunch. Tiny bells ringing to receive blessings.

But one sound resonated above all others. It was a deep and rich "Ommm." I knew whose voice that chant belonged to, but I couldn't quite believe it. When I opened my eyes, there was Sastry, gazing warmly back at me.

It had been well over twenty years since I last saw him, but he looked almost exactly the same. His soulful eyes, his radiant smile.

Sastry and I embraced, then sat down in the same exact spot we had when I was a kid. He asked me about myself—about what I'd done with my life.

I told Sastry my story. How I had spent too long pursuing a path that didn't feel like my own. I told him how I had attempted to change things, trying so hard to discover and express my essence.

As the words poured out of me, so did the emotion. My lips quivered, my voice grew shaky, and tears streamed down my cheeks. Sastry was a man I had always admired, and I wanted nothing more than for him to be proud of me. To believe that I had lived up to the potential he once saw.

But I hadn't.

"I'm lost, Sastry," I said. "I tried to live my dharma . . . but I failed."

Sastry held my gaze and sat with me in silence. He took a deep inhale and closed his eyes, searching his soul for the right words.

"Suneel," he said. "It is *always* better to fail at your own dharma than to succeed at someone else's."

That day Sastry became my teacher once again. We talked about the actions we take, win or lose, in the spirit of our own essence. How action doesn't always lead to achievement—but if it's in line with your dharma, it will always bring you closer to who you really are. And from that new place inside, possibilities arise. Possibilities you couldn't have seen before.

Through these conversations with Sastry, I began to realize that coming home was about more than running for office. It was about reconnecting with a part of myself that I had left behind— not just in Detroit, but on a porch in New Delhi.

Losing an election led me back to my temple, back to my roots, and ultimately to the path of writing this book.

For much of my life, I believed that dharma was a series of steps to climb. Now I know that dharma isn't a hill, but a cycle. It's the wheel that Bauji drew on his porch.

In this Wheel of Dharma, you win, you lose—you win, you lose. The cycle never stops, but with every turn you become more aware of who you are and how you want to show up in the world. Your character builds, your compass sharpens, and your courage deepens for that next trip around the wheel.

WHERE WE BEGIN AGAIN

Whether you realize it yet or not, your dharma has already come alive inside of you. You're going to start noticing changes in your creativity and aspiration. You'll see shifts in the way you make choices, serve others, and respond to challenges.

Be assured that you've changed, that you're a different person now.

You understand what it means to have an essence, which is deeper than an occupation and free from the need for outside approval. You have four tools in hand to chisel away the cruft and bring you back to your core.

You see how your duties can actually fuel your dharma—and how your dharma can fuel your duties. You get that it's far better to be full-hearted and half scheduled than fully scheduled and half-hearted.

You know how energy and dharma are intertwined. That when you embrace rhythmic renewal instead of incessant grit, you hitch your wagon to a bottomless source of power.

You're able to find comfort in the discomfort—the tiny space between impulse and response that, when opened just a tad, can give you back your freedom.

And you're not playing the Game of Someday—you're playing the Game of Now. You're no longer waiting for courage to take action. You're taking action and letting courage catch up along the way.

Throughout our journey together, we have learned over thirty different lessons and rituals. That's a lot to soak in. I have a daily mantra, inspired by Ram Dass, that helps me bring it all together.

Love. Serve. Believe.

Love the part of you that wants nothing more than to express itself to the world. Spend one-on-one time with your dharma each day. Listen to it with an open heart. Take it everywhere you go, even into parts of your life that seem unrelated. Remember that your essence has been with you from the start and will always be a part of you. Loving it is the same as loving yourself.

Then, lose yourself in service and switch the spotlight from yourself to others. Embrace your ambition and shed your expectations. Service is the purest form of expression. When you shift the focus to others, you turn your dharma into a mission and become more dedicated to it than you ever thought possible.

And finally, believe. Believe that when you're in your dharma, you've already won. This doesn't mean you always succeed, but you always learn and you always grow.

Love, serve, believe—each one fuels the other. The more you love, the more capacity you have to serve others. The more you serve, the more you believe in your ability to express your essence to the world. Which brings you back to a feeling of love. You're doing what you love—and loving what you do.

There are so many things in life that can weigh us down. The *love, serve, believe* cycle will always lift us back up.

We began our journey with a simple idea. Outer success (wealth, status, and achievement) is unlikely to ever lead us to inner success (lasting joy, fulfillment, personal growth).

But you can reverse the flow. If you begin with inner success— if you *love, serve,* and *believe* in that place inside—then you are on a path to outer success as well.

Bauji once told me that God strums a sitar with billions of strings. Each of us is a string, and each strum plays the sound of our collective dharma.

If your string is out of tune, it affects everyone else's song. By living your dharma, you're doing your part to bring the rest of the world into harmony.

When my mom was scared to get on a boat to America, it was the story of Uncle Tulsi's keys that gave her hope. Whenever my cousins find themselves a little down, they do one of Harkrishan's shoulder shakes to lift their spirits. When I'm afraid to step up onstage, I imagine Nani sitting on a dirt floor, summoning the courage to sing for Mahatma Gandhi.

As I was finishing up this book, my ten-year-old daughter, Sammy, decided to try out for the local dance team. Sammy loves music, and she loves to perform. So it felt poetic for me to be writing about dharma while watching my daughter embrace hers.

Parents weren't allowed to go inside and watch the tryouts, but I could at least serve as transportation on her big day.

I waited outside of Sammy's school, eager for the excitement we were about to share. But when she came out, her shoulders were slumped, and her gaze was to the ground. She quietly got in the car and buckled herself in.

On our drive to the studio, Sammy opened up. She told me how scared she was to try out. How afraid she was to be judged by adults and to mess up in front of her friends. Most of all, she was terrified to find out that she hadn't made the team. To find out that dancing wasn't her dharma after all.

I desperately wanted to tell her something that would lift her confidence. Something that would make her understand that music *is* her essence. I wanted to tell her how as a baby she would perk up the moment a song began to play. How her eyes would brighten when we danced around the kitchen counter.

Before I got a single word out, I saw her face in the rearview mirror. Tears were rolling down her cheeks, and her tiny hands were trembling. All I wanted to do was make her feel okay.

Had she simply said "I don't want to do this anymore," I would have U-turned the car and taken her home to safety. Despite her tears, those words never came. So we just kept driving toward the studio.

We pulled into a parking lot inside the strip mall, and before I knew it, she was out of the car. I watched her through the window as she wiped her cheeks, walked into the building, and closed the door behind her.

My little girl was gone.

At the moment my daughter needed me the most, I wasn't able to retrieve any of the wisdom inside this book. The next forty-five minutes were some of the most agonizing I've felt as a father. But at least I knew what I wanted to say when she returned, the dharma lessons I was now prepared to share.

When Sammy reemerged from the studio, everything about her was different. She was confident and poised. There was a pep in her step.

When she got into the car, I blurted out, "So you made the team?" She looked at me, smiled, and shrugged her shoulders. "I don't know, Dad. We won't find out for another couple of days."

Sammy wasn't experiencing outer success at that moment. She was experiencing inner success. When you're expressing your essence, you don't need an achievement or an accolade or even a spot on the dance roster to validate your dreams. You can feel it. You know it.

If you look hard enough at your own story, you'll find a moment that feels like the true beginning. Like the start of your dharma journey. Maybe it was the moment you decided to make a change, to take a stand, to try something new. Or maybe that moment is right now.

For me, it will always be those early mornings in New Delhi with my grandfather. Long after I left, Bauji continued his tradition on that porch, his hands gently wrapped around a hot mug of chai, watching his city wake up. So much had changed over the course of his life, and yet fruit cart vendors still bellowed prices into the open air, rickshaws still fired their engines for the day ahead, and the Wheel of Dharma was still at the center of every Indian flag.

On the last morning of his life, Bauji sat in stillness.

He noticed everything that had changed about India, and all those special little things that never would, until that mug of chai slowly slipped from his hands.

I think of my grandfather every morning as I sit on my front porch holding a hot cup of coffee. Sometimes my daughers, Sammy and Serena, join me outside, just as I would join Bauji.

Only now, they're the ones giving *me* the curious look, and I'm the one with my feet pressed firmly into the ground.

One day I'll hand this book to them. One day I'll share with them everything I've learned about dharma. For now, we sit in silence, side by side, watching our neighborhood wake up.

And then, without fail, I lift my finger and slowly begin to draw the shape of an imaginary wheel. They know what's coming, and their faces light up in anticipation. I trace and retrace the circle, each time going faster and faster until I'm rounding the wheel like a maniac. My seriousness has shifted to play, and their eyes begin to smile. I let out a chuckle, and they break out into belly laughs.

I wrap my arms around them, pull them in close. Then I whisper something into their ears.

"We must always find our way back to the center."

Bauji and me at his home in New Delhi

ACKNOWLEDGMENTS

During a visit to America, Swami Satchidananda was asked about the difference between "illness" and "wellness." Satchidananda wrote both words on a blackboard, then circled the "i" in illness and the "we" in wellness.

It is difficult to name, let alone thank, all the people who helped bring this book to health.

Robin Rice, Stephen Cope, Tony D'Amelio and the DN team, Jonny Kest, Andy Mahoney, Jon Polk, Megan Elder, Clayton Ruebensaal, Tommy Harper, Nico Carbonaro, Jon Campbell, Keenan Newman, Daniel Pink, David Vigliano, Ian Salvage, Hilary Illick, Marissa Ingrasci, Steve Mosko, Reid Hoffman, John Lilly, Greg Rudin, Arun Paul, Ashok Krishnaswamy—the list goes on.

Thank you, Gideon Weil, Maya Alpert, Daniella Wexler, Judith Curr, Lucile Culver, Melinda Mullin, and the rest of the HarperOne team for taking a chance on me. I know this book wasn't an obvious bet, and I hope it makes you proud.

Thank you, Dikran Ornekian, for breathing life into these pages. It's a rare gift in life when your creative collaborator is also your best friend. From the day we graduated, you've known who you are, and how you want to express that to the world. You've never strayed, never lost sight of what matters to you. There's no one with whom I'd rather walk this path of purpose.

Thank you, Mom and Dad, for keeping these stories sacred and for sharing them with me when I needed them most. Since I was a child, you never stopped encouraging me to play the Game of Now. Thank you, Sanjay, for being an everyday reminder of what can happen when someone fully steps into their dharma.

Thank you, Leena, for believing in me. For *really* believing in me. If there were a ninth chapter of this book, it would be a love letter to you. So much of our dharma is shaped by our partners in life. So many times I lost my way—and without fail, you were there to guide me back. I am who I am because of you.

Thank you, Sammy and Serena, for filling my life with meaning and joy. For the past three years of writing this book, all I could think about was you. One day, when you leave the house, I hope this book can be a companion on your path. The stories inside are of the people who lived their dharma so that you could one day live yours.

SUKHA

Kleck, Robert E., and A. Christopher Strenta. "Gender and Responses to Disfigurement in Self and Others." *Personality and Social Psychology Bulletin* 14, no. 2 (1988): 365–72. doi: 10.1177/0146167288142016.

BHAKTI

Belton, Teresa, and Esther Priyadharshini. "Boredom and Schooling: A Cross-Disciplinary Exploration." *Cambridge Journal of Education* 37, no. 4 (2007): 579–95. doi: 10.1080/03057640701706227.

Fox, Margalit. "Toni Morrison, Towering Novelist of the Black Experience, Dies at 88." *New York Times*, August 6, 2019. https://www.nytimes.com/2019/08/06/books/toni-morrison-dead.html.

Gelb, Michael. *How to Think Like Leonardo da Vinci: Seven Steps to Genius Every Day*. Delta, 2004, 109.

Morrison, Toni. "Toni Morrison Reflects on Her Powerful Turning Point as a Writer." YouTube video, 2:11. Posted by OWN, April 6, 2015.

PRANA

Albulescu, P., I. Macsinga, A. Rusu, C. Sulea, A. Bodnaru, and B. T. Tulbure. "'Give me a break!' A Systematic Review and Meta-Analysis on the Efficacy of Micro-Breaks for Increasing Well-Being and Performance." *PLOS ONE* 17, no. 8 (2022): e0272460. https://doi .org/10.1371/journal.pone.0272460.

Cleveland Clinic. "Brain Facts." https://healthybrains.org/brain-facts.

Comaford, Christine. "Got Inner Peace? 5 Ways to Get It Now." Forbes, April 4, 2012. https://www.forbes.com/sites/christinecomaford/2012 /04/04/got-inner-peace-5-ways-to-get-it-now/.

Murphy, Joseph. "How to Use the Power of Your Subconscious Mind." Chap. 6 in *The Power of Your Subconscious Mind*, 70. Prentice Hall Press, 2008.

Sievertsen, H. H., F. Gino, and M. Piovesan. "Cognitive Fatigue Influences Students' Performance on Standardized Tests." *Proceedings of the National Academy of Sciences of the United States of America* 113, no. 10 (2016): 2621–24. doi: 10.1073/pnas.1516947113.

Sonnentag, S. "The Recovery Paradox: Portraying the Complex Interplay Between Job Stressors, Lack of Recovery, and Poor Well-Being." *Research in Organizational Behavior* 38 (2018): 169–85. https:// doi.org/10.1016/j.riob.2018.11.002.

University of Alberta. "Morning People and Night Owls Show Different Brain Function." *ScienceDaily*. www.sciencedaily.com/releases /2009/06/090623150621.htm (accessed May 8, 2023).

LEELA

Biderman, David. "'The Africans Are Hearing Footsteps: Kara Goucher Leads a U.S. Marathon Revival; Her Style—Run More, Think Less." *Wall Street Journal*, August 21, 2009.

Hendrix, Jimi, and Nancy Carter. "Jimi Hendrix June 1969 Interview." Podcast interview. Posted by Rebel Without a Cause, September 16, 2020.

Jackson, Phil. *Sacred Hoops*. Hachette Books, 1996, 123.

McDougall, Christopher. *Born to Run: A Hidden Tribe, Superathletes, and the Greatest Race the World Has Never Seen*. New York: Alfred A. Knopf, 2009, 70–72, 79–83, 102–7.

Viesturs, Ed. "Endgame on Everest." *Outside*, May 1997, 52–62.

SEVA

Friend, Tad. "The One Who Knocks." *The New Yorker*, September 9, 2013.

Guha, Ramachandra. *Gandhi: The Years That Changed the World, 1914–1948*. Knopf Doubleday Publishing Group, 2018, 330.

TULA

Avgoustaki, A. and Frankort, Hans T. W. "Implications of Work Effort and Discretion for Employee Well-Being and Career-Related Outcomes: An Integrative Assessment." *Industrial and Labor Relations Review* 72, no. 3 (2019): 636–61. doi: 10.1177/0019793918804540.

KRIYA

Bezos, Jeff. "2017 Letter to Shareholders." Amazon, April 12, 2018. https://www.sec.gov/Archives/edgar/data/1018724/000119312516530910/d168744dex991.htm.

Gallup. "State of the American Workplace: Employee Engagement Insights for U.S. Business Leaders." Gallup, 2013. https://www.gallup.com/workplace/238079/state-american-workplace-report-2017.aspx.

Kahneman, Daniel, and Amos Tversky. "Prospect Theory: An Analysis of Decision Making under Risk." *Econometrica* 47 (1979): 263–91. http://dx.doi.org/10.2307/1914185.

Pink, Daniel H. *Drive: The Surprising Truth About What Motivates Us.* Riverhead Books, 2009.

The Conference Board. "U.S. Job Satisfaction Declines to Record Low." 2010. Retrieved from https://www.conference-board.org/press/pressdetail.cfm?pressid=4252.

ABOUT THE AUTHOR

After losing touch with his dharma, Suneel Gupta went on a journey to find it again. As the cofounder of RISE and a visiting scholar at Harvard Medical School, Suneel travels the world, deconstructing how extraordinary performers overcome their most difficult moments. His work has been featured by *Vanity Fair, Fast Company,* and the *New York Times.*